THANK YOU,
GOD

COUNT YOUR
DAILY BLESSINGS

Publications International, Ltd.

Louis Weber, CEO
Publications International, Ltd.
7373 North Cicero Avenue
Lincolnwood, Illinois 60712

8 7 6 5 4 3 2 1

ISBN: 1-4127-1126-6

Contents

Gratitude Is the Key

*T*here is something magical about counting your blessings, for just by focusing your attention on the good things in your life, you suddenly start to see even more blessings appear. It's as if a switch has been turned on, clearing the way for greater good to flow toward you.

That switch is the act of gratitude, for when you turn to God in praise and thanks, God responds by opening your eyes and heart to the infinite blessings that you may have overlooked before. Suddenly, life is filled with wonders too numerous to count. The abundance of the universe takes your breath away. You realize that you are literally immersed in the miraculous.

In this beautiful and inspiring book, you will find a collection of quotes, poems, stories, and meditations about the many ways God blesses our lives. You will celebrate the joys of being with family and the priceless treasures of having friendships. You will recognize those special blessings that come from unexpected people, events, and random acts of kindness. You will feel the pride and spirit of home and community. You will cherish the healing power and splendor of nature; the lessons to be found in life's biggest challenges; and the happiness that comes from living in the moment, when miracles appear in the tiniest of details. You will revel in the fulfillment that comes from being who you are and using your unique gifts and talents. Both spring from the deep connection you share with a God who loves you and shows you that love in countless ways each and every day.

This book is a gift that will transform you in profound and wondrous ways. For if you have ever felt as though your life was lacking in any way, the sayings and poems and stories included in these pages will change your perception and awaken your spirit to the multitude of blessings, both big and small, that already exist around you.

Embrace the gift. Count your blessings. Just say, "Thank You, God." Then watch those marvelous blessings multiply.

Chapter One

The Joy of Family

Family is the precious gift of human angels sent to love, support, and guide us.

We may not be able to choose our family members the way we choose our friends,

> We know that we can accomplish anything and overcome any challenge in life when we have the love and support of our family. Suddenly, we are given the faith and belief in ourselves upon which our dreams, our goals, and our visions take flight. With family beside us, we can walk through fire, climb every mountain, and soar to the highest peaks. They are both our foundation and our wings.

but God knows best what is necessary for us to truly learn the lessons of life that we were sent here to learn. And what better

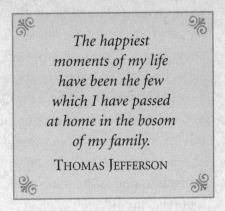

The happiest moments of my life have been the few which I have passed at home in the bosom of my family.

THOMAS JEFFERSON

way to teach us those lessons than by placing us in the midst of families filled with different characters, opinions, and ideas; families that challenge us, encourage us, and push us to dare to be who we really are and to go after our dreams even when we are not sure we have it in us.

By being a part of a family, we come to understand the blessings of connection, communication, tolerance, acceptance, interaction, humility, and love. Our relatives care for us, guide us, protect us, and support us, but sometimes they provoke us and push our buttons. Maybe some of them even enrage us, but those family members may end up being our most important teachers.

No matter what they do, our families never cease to serve as powerful guides and guardians in our lives; pillars of strength to hold us up when we are weak; models of character we strive to emulate as we grow older; and wise sages to direct us when we are lost and alone.

An old proverb says because God couldn't be everywhere at once, he gave us families to carry out his work. They are our angels, and we are angels to them as well. This give-and-take relationship is one of the many blessings family members provide.

Only God's love is forever, but family members come a close second. They are the cornerstones of our foundations and the stars in the sky urging us to reach ever higher. So let us thank God for them.

—◄O►—

God, bless my family,
each and every one,
for without them I would be lost.
Their love sustains me;
their belief in me holds me up when
I cannot walk alone. Thank you, God,
for the gift of my family.
Amen

—◄O►—

No Such Thing as Being Alone

Katy had lived in the same community as most of her extended family all her life. Now, at 25, she was moving 2,000 miles away to where her husband's job had relocated him. They had to make the move; good jobs like her husband's were getting scarce, and his company provided great benefits, retirement savings, and plenty of paid days off for family time.

Nevertheless, for Katy, all those benefits didn't make it any easier. She was very close to her mom and dad, her brother Kerry and his wife, Anita, and she was the favorite auntie to her brother's little Anna. In their new location, Katy wouldn't know a soul, and it would mean making new friends all over again, something she was not adept at. But her husband had promised

> *Above all, clothe yourselves with love, which binds everything together in perfect harmony. And let the peace of Christ rule in your hearts, to which indeed you were called in the one body. And be thankful.*
>
> COLOSSIANS 3:14–15

her they would move back to be near her family once they decided to have children. Until then, she would sweat it out in a strange town with unfamiliar

> *Those we call family love us no matter what we do right or what we do wrong. They are bound to us by more than just blood. They are bound to us in spirit.*

people and no one to call "family."

The day of the move came very quickly, and Katy decided to grin and bear it as best she could. They had planned to drive cross-country, staying in hotels in several states she and her husband had always wanted to see. Once they arrived in their new town, Katy could barely hold back her tears.

Their new house was lovely, and the neighborhood seemed nice. After their furniture arrived, they kept themselves busy organizing their new home to make it a place where they could feel comfortable. Exhausted, Katy could barely stand up as she plugged the phone into the outlet. Within seconds, it rang.

First, it was her mom and dad, calling just to say hi and see how she was doing. Within moments of hanging up, the phone rang again, and it was her brother and his family. She spent about 20 minutes with them and then hung up. Two minutes later—exactly—her neighbor from back home called to wish her well. Then an aunt who lived in another state called to say hi, followed by Katy's grandmother and her husband's mom and sister.

Two hours later, Katy finally got to the bathroom for her shower without a phone call interrupting her. As she came out, she passed the room they would use as a home office, and her husband called her into the room. He had arranged ahead of time for their Internet service to be up and running, and he had a huge smile on his face when he told Katy to check her e-mail. She was stunned to find more than a dozen messages from family members, including pictures of them waving and holding signs that read, "You can never get rid of us!"

Katy's face lit up with a huge smile. She and her husband had been blessed with loving family members, and she silently thanked God for helping her understand that she was never really alone. In fact, she would always be just a phone call or e-mail away from the ones she adored. The thought made her heart swell, and she felt so good that she went outside to bask in the warm sun. As she stood in their front yard, a woman about her age holding a newborn baby came up and introduced herself as one of Katy's neighbors. She welcomed Katy to the community, and Katy knew that she was going to like her new home after all. More importantly, she thanked God that family was about the heart and not geography.

Heavenly Father, today I ask you to bless those that I love and call my family. Guard and guide them as they go about their days. Shelter and protect them from harm. Love them and care for them. This I ask of you, Lord.
Amen

Dreamweaver

Uncle Joe was always Gina's favorite relative. He would sit and read the most imaginative stories to her. They would be wild adventures with Gina as the lead character. Gina cherished those special times and stories so much that she begged Uncle Joe to let her have the stories when she was older.

They shall again live beneath my shadow,
they shall flourish as a garden; they shall
blossom like the vine, their fragrance shall
be like the wine of Lebanon.

HOSEA 14:7

But when Gina turned ten, her Uncle Joe died of a heart attack, leaving her feeling lost and alone. She loved her parents, but nobody understood her like Uncle Joe. He knew about Gina's dream of being a writer, and he never once tried to discourage her by saying that it was a bad career choice or that writers didn't always make a good living.

By the time Gina was in her late 20s, she was working as an accountant, making great money but drinking so much when she got home that she often went to work the next day with a hangover. On one of her worst days, Gina went straight home and opened a bottle of wine, drowning herself in her pain. She hated her job, and worse still, she hated herself for selling out her dream so many years ago.

The doorbell to her apartment rang, and Gina opened the door. A deliveryperson handed her a large box. Gina was surprised to see that the box was from her Aunt Jane, Uncle Joe's widow. She opened it and lifted out a batch of bound manuscripts.

As Gina flipped through the manuscripts, she began to cry. They were short stories, written by her uncle, the very same stories he used to read to her! Gina realized, all these years later, that her uncle had been a writer and that those special stories had been his own creations.

A note fluttered to the ground, and Gina picked it up. It was from her Aunt Jane.

"I found these in the attic. Your Uncle Joe loved to write, and he loved you. You were the daughter he always wanted, and he would have wanted you to have these. Love, Aunt Jane."

Gina sat for more than an hour, deep in thought, and then she did what she should have done years ago when she knew exactly who she was and what she wanted to be.

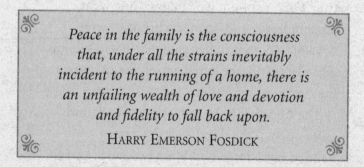

Peace in the family is the consciousness that, under all the strains inevitably incident to the running of a home, there is an unfailing wealth of love and devotion and fidelity to fall back upon.

HARRY EMERSON FOSDICK

My Dream Team

If at first I don't succeed
Or fail to get the things I need,
My family is there for me,
To cheer me on and care for me.
Like angels sent from God above
They lift me up on wings of love.
They give me faith to try anew
And do the things I long to do.

Pulling out her laptop computer, Gina began to write. The next day, she told her boss she wanted to work part-time. She had a dream, and she was committing herself to it. She knew God had given her a double blessing: the gift of a loving uncle who wanted her to dream big and the security of a large savings account. She may have hated her job, but now she thanked God for the financial cushion it would give her.

Gina called her mom and dad and told them about her decision. She was surprised to find that they fully supported her. That night, Gina went to bed sober for the first time in a long time, and she prayed, offering God her deepest gratitude for opening her eyes to the love and support that was always there for her.

Instant Family

I had always thought Rick and I would have a family of our own, but when my doctor informed me that I could never safely give birth because of a past surgery, I was devastated. My dreams of a house filled with giggling children were shattered, and Rob was crushed.

My sister had adopted her third child, after having two of her own, and quietly suggested that Rick and I consider doing the same. I was so buried in my own bitterness and grief, so angry at God for not letting me become a "real" mom, that I couldn't even think about it. But as time went on, and I saw how my sister's little girl fit in with her natural family as if she had been born into it, the idea of adoption made more and more sense.

Rick agreed, and within nine months, we had adopted 18-month-old twins, a boy and girl, abandoned by their teenage mother. We fell in love with them at first sight, and we were the only couple the agency knew of willing to take on two children at once.

For the first few months, I felt extremely torn between the joy of finally having my family and my feelings of separateness and lack of connection with these two babies. I fed and bathed them. I changed their diapers and went through all the motions of being a mom, but something was missing, and I could tell Rick was going through the same struggle. We loved our new children, but we felt as though they still really belonged to someone else.

My sister gave us her support and her wisdom, for she had experienced the same thing. "Give it time," she would say, assuring us that we would one day become convinced that we and we alone were their mom and dad. I had thanked God so many times for giving us these beautiful babies, and now I was back praying that he would open our hearts to accept these babies as our own flesh and spirit.

It happened about a week later when Rick and I were playing with the babies and they both looked at me and simultaneously said, "Mama." I broke down and cried in Rick's arms. It sounded so perfect, so natural, so meant to be. Rick was a

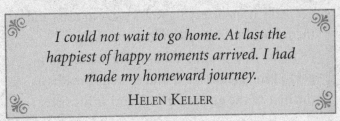

I could not wait to go home. At last the happiest of happy moments arrived. I had made my homeward journey.

HELEN KELLER

bit jealous, but the babies did try to say "Dada," only it came out more like "Dayday," and we laughed and cried and thanked God together for his blessings of the real family we had dreamed of, and for the wisdom of a sister who knew all good things would come in time.

Dear God, I know I sometimes complain about my family, especially those certain members who really know how to push my buttons, but I truly give thanks for each and every one of them, and for the love they give, and the lessons they teach.
Amen

Pushing Buttons

Rob hated these family get-togethers. It never failed that his sister's husband Alan would pick an argument with Rob about the differences in their political beliefs. Usually the conversations would get really heated, leaving Rob's sister in tears and the rest of the family wanting to go home.

Today Rob promised he would not let Alan get to him. He took a few deep belly breaths as the first of the guests arrived, and as his sister

SHARING EVERYTHING

Families share more than just last names.
They share hopes, dreams, goals, and cares.
They share worries, angers, doubts, and grief,
They commiserate in all their fears.
They share up days and down days
and in between,
They share laughter, gossip, jokes, and song.
They share trivia, triumphs, trials, and travails,
And they stick like glue when things go wrong.

and Alan walked in, he was feeling firmly grounded. But within minutes, Alan was all over him, breathing his awful beer breath in Rob's face and yelling in his ear about some political mumbo jumbo.

Rob stood his ground, trying his best to just ignore Alan and instead busied himself with preparing the grill. But everywhere he went, Alan followed, bellowing about how Rob and his "ilk" were ruining the country. Rob could see his sister cringing in a corner, and by the pleading look in her eyes, he knew a confrontation would only make matters worst.

Finally, Rob let his cousin Jim take over the grill while he snuck off to use the bathroom. He

> *We may not like every single one of our relatives, but each of them has a gift to offer us, especially those we call "difficult." For it is easy to understand and get along with those we have much in common with, but learning to understand and get along with those unlike us is truly an empowering lesson.*

used the quiet time to think carefully about the situation. *Okay,* he thought, *I have two ways I can react. Either continue to ignore Alan, which will make him yell only louder, or confront him, which will ruin the barbecue.*

Rob silently prayed to God for the courage and the wisdom to do the highest and best thing. He thanked God for the answer, which he didn't know yet, but he knew the answer would arrive when he needed it. God had never let him down.

Outside, Alan complained about how Rob should switch political parties and stop being a fool. Rob turned to Alan and did something that surprised everyone at the party. He gave his brother-in-law a full bear hug, and, with a huge smile, said, "What would a party be without you, buddy!"

Alan stood there, speechless, and Rob thanked God again for that blessing alone! From that point on, Alan was much quieter and subdued. Rob continued to smile each time he passed Alan, patting him on the back, and at one point thanking Alan for helping him to see things from a different perspective.

Even as Rob said the words, he realized it was true. Alan was a blessing, not a curse, for by pushing Rob's buttons, he helped Rob closely examine his own beliefs. Could he even come to like Alan? He knew God worked in mysterious ways...but this was ridiculous! With a wink skyward to thank God for coming through, Rob returned his attention to the grill.

Stuck Like Glue

Having her sister so close by meant the world to Becky. She and Ricki were only two years apart, but most people thought they were twins. They were downright inseparable. So it was only natural that Ricki offer her kid sister the gift of life itself when Becky was diagnosed with a form

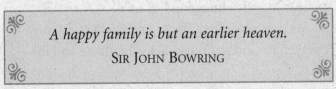

A happy family is but an earlier heaven.
SIR JOHN BOWRING

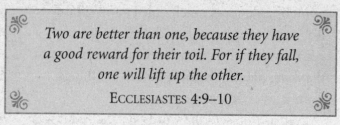

> *Two are better than one, because they have*
> *a good reward for their toil. For if they fall,*
> *one will lift up the other.*
>
> ECCLESIASTES 4:9–10

of leukemia that would require a complete bone marrow transplant.

Ricki had been first in line to be tested for a match, and she had prayed to God to make her the one that Becky could rely on. Sure enough, God answered her prayers, and within two months, Ricki and Becky entered the hospital and the procedure went off without a hitch. Becky later joked to the nurses how she just couldn't get rid of her sister, that they were "stuck like glue," literally!

For the months that followed, the two sisters stuck by each other through the painful and slow recovery period. When Becky came down with an infection that could jeopardize her improving health, Ricki was there. When Ricki suffered severe pain from the bone marrow removal procedure and could barely move, Becky was by her side with warm hugs and hot cocoa.

As they recovered, Becky and Ricki constantly prayed to God in gratitude for his grace and his love, but mostly they thanked him for making them sisters and best friends. Both women realized that nothing was more important in the entire world than the love of family, a love they now truly believed could carry them through any tragedy, challenge, or disaster.

When their mother died one year later, the two sisters grieved together and helped the rest of their large family cope. Becky would tell Ricki day after day how grateful she was for her, and Ricki did likewise. Their love for each other gave them the courage and the strength they needed to help their father prepare for the funeral and work through his own grief.

But mostly it was their love for God, and their awareness of his blessings that carried them all through this tragic time, keeping their eyes and hearts focused on the brighter days to come.

· ◆ ►◄O►◄ ◆ ·

God, I come to you today in thanks and praise
for giving me my family. They love and support
me and allow me to dream big. With this
wonderful family you have given me, I know that
I can do anything, and for that I am grateful.
Amen

· ◆ ►◄O►◄ ◆ ·

Chapter Two

The Treasure of Friendship

Friendship is a priceless blessing from God.

I remember the lyrics of a Brownie Scout song we sang at every meeting: "Make new friends but keep the old; one is silver and the other's gold." My troop of long-forgotten little girls is probably scattered all over the United States by now and perhaps all over the world, but I believe we share the spirit of friendship and that those lyrics are hardwired into our hearts. I would bet that 90 percent of the women

> *Beloved, let us love one another, because love is from God; everyone who loves is born of God and knows God.*
>
> 1JOHN 4:7

reading this paragraph are humming that song right now.

We hum it because the song we learned as little girls has proven to be true. New friendships may bloom and then fade. They meant the world to us for a time, but we moved on and apart from those friends. Old friends, however, are gold, never fading and never failing to shine for us. Old friends are rare, and we can count them among our greatest treasures.

◆━◇━◆

Thank you, God, for blessing me with friends who share my triumphs without jealousy, my challenges with cheerleading, and my dark paths with the light of their companionship. I especially thank you for their honesty even when it hurts to hear it. Help me be as good a friend to them as they are to me.

◆━◇━◆

No Greater Love

Tom was my first best friend, and though many wonderful people have crossed my path since I knew him, not one has lived up to the example that he set. Forty years after our last meeting, my love and admiration for Tom remain stronger than ever.

We met at school at the age of five and soon became best pals. Both of us were learning to play the piano, and it was our mutual love of music that brought us together. For the next seven years we were almost inseparable, forever

In the chapel of Santa Croce Church in Rome, I stare at a nail said to be used in the crucifixion of Christ. Me, staring, when all my life I've avoided Good Friday, unwilling to encounter such pain. The nail is blunt at the business end and big for a nail. My friend Joan kneels with me and holds my hand. She whispers a line of a hymn: "Were you there when they nailed him to the tree?" Yes, but with my friend. I can't kneel at Calvary alone.

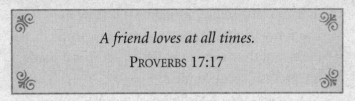

A friend loves at all times.

PROVERBS 17:17

hammering away at the keys of my mother's baby grand.

Tom was a great piano player. I was small for my age and had trouble reaching the pedals, but his legs were just the right length for my mother's piano stool. We were supposed to be studying the classic composers, like Beethoven and Mozart, but Tom loved to stretch his fingers toward the black keys and start jazzing around. Sometimes it was hard to figure out where Beethoven stopped and Count Basie began once Tom really got going. I loved to sit with a glass of lemonade and listen to Tom play. It was a joy to be so young, happy, and carefree.

But those joyous, carefree days ended when we reached the age of ten. We were packed off to a new school, and we both encountered troubles when we got there.

I was still small and became an easy target for a fiendish pair of bullies. They stole my lunch and pulled my hair, but what hurt the most were the verbal insults. As soon as I got to school each morning, the bullies would start teasing me about my height. I tried to argue back with them, but they were so much bigger that it made my protests seem comical.

Tom was the one who saved me. And considering what he was going through, his friendship and loyalty were all the more remarkable. Soon after we got to our new school, Tom had been diagnosed with sickle-cell anemia, a rare blood disease. When a victim of the disease is wounded, the deficiencies in the blood mean that it doesn't clot properly. Even the smallest cut becomes potentially life-threatening.

Tom and I were walking home from school one day when the two bullies jumped me from behind. They dragged me into some bushes and started to beat me up. Soon I was crying, which the bullies loved to see me do.

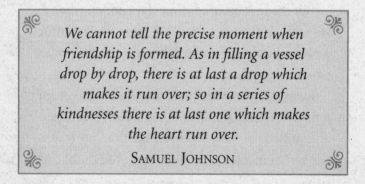

We cannot tell the precise moment when friendship is formed. As in filling a vessel drop by drop, there is at last a drop which makes it run over; so in a series of kindnesses there is at last one which makes the heart run over.

SAMUEL JOHNSON

"Let go of him," Tom demanded.

"Buzz off," one of the bullies told him. "This is between us."

Tom didn't budge an inch. "Pick on someone your own size," he said defiantly. "Stephen might not be as big as you guys, but he's 50 times the person you'll ever be. If you lay another finger on him, I'll hit you so hard…"

It was amazing. He didn't even have to finish the sentence. The bullies just ran off. I've read many times that bullies are secretly cowards, but at the time neither Tom nor I knew that.

We lost touch a year later when my family moved away. I hadn't seen Tom for more than 12 years when I received a letter from his mother saying that the disease had finally taken him. He had passed away peacefully and had asked to be remembered by me.

Reading that letter, I felt like the kid that had known and needed Tom all those years ago. I felt like a helpless ten-year-old again as tears poured down my cheeks.

Tom, you will stay in my heart forever, and I will never stop praising God for the way you risked your life to save me. God bless you, Tom, and thank you for being a true friend.

On the Back Porch

"Just remember, dear. We went through puberty together," my friend Deanna said, stirring a little sugar in her iced tea on my back porch.

"And menopause," I said.

"Three divorces." She squeezed a little lemon juice in her tea and squeezed the rest into my glass. She dipped the rind in the sugar bowl. My Jack Russell terrier puppy, Maggie, eagerly "sat" for her treat of sugarcoated lemon rind.

"So many secrets," I said with a sigh.

"We should number them," she said, "like comics do jokes. Shout out the number instead of going through the whole joke. Then we can laugh after each number."

◆—◆—◀O▶—◆—◆

Dear God, help me be a good friend to those who need me today. Nudge me toward the phone, or to my note cards, or to my car, and tell me what to do or say. And when and where and how. You have been such a good friend to me. Help me do for others, especially my friends, what you have done for me. I cannot do it with such loving selflessness without your help. Amen

◆—◆—◀O▶—◆—◆

"Some of our secrets aren't so funny," I said.

We were quiet for a moment. Solemn and sober. We did not need to name our secrets or number them. Some were funny. Some were sad. The day we knocked over the Christmas tree and blamed it on her family's poodle. Her failed suicide attempt after her husband left her. My failed car arson attempt when I found out my husband was unfaithful. Those first gray hairs.

Maggie broke our pensive mood by leaping on Deanna's lap for another treat. She gave the dog an unsweetened lemon slice. "That's life, Maggie. Deal with it." Maggie slunk under my chair and moped.

Deanna laughed. "She is clueless. She'll never know the pain of labor, the joy of birth, the right brand of hair dye." She bent down and looked Maggie in the face. "Maggie," she said, "we have stretch marks, fake blonde hair, and FOUR CHILDREN!"

"Five children," I said.

Deanna sat back in her chair and looked at me with love and sorrow in her eyes.

"You are the only person in this world who ever mentions Erin," she said. "You are the only person in this world besides me who ever thinks of her."

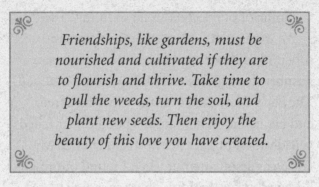

> *Friendships, like gardens, must be*
> *nourished and cultivated if they are*
> *to flourish and thrive. Take time to*
> *pull the weeds, turn the soil, and*
> *plant new seeds. Then enjoy the*
> *beauty of this love you have created.*

It was 40 years ago that Deanna's first child was born. Erin was born prematurely and died within hours. I was not a mother yet, but I had held my friend's hand and tried to help shoulder her pain. We held a private funeral, just Deanna and me and the pastor, and the tiny, white coffin. The baby's father was a helicopter pilot posted overseas.

Maggie jumped back on Deanna's lap and licked a small tear from her cheek.

"I think I'll get a little dog," she said. "Maggie is such good company."

"Do that," I said. "We can go through dog obedience school together."

"Sounds easier than puberty," she said.

And it was.

Each day I thank God for Deanna's friendship. We have a special bond that God has formed from the tears and joys we have shared together through the many years.

From Sweet 16 to Frankly 40

My teenage daughter and her best girlfriend surprised me one day by asking to borrow my old dictionary for a homework assignment. Didn't kids do everything online these days? I knew her computer had an online dictionary because I had installed it myself. I was busy whipping egg whites, so I nodded and pointed to the middle shelf of the bookcase. I was tempted to ask, "Do you know how to use reference materials with hard covers?" but I did not want to hear "Oh mother, really!" again today.

Yet the question hung around my kitchen until I heard giggles from her bedroom, then laughter. They had probably found a new word for a private body part. I smiled, recalling a few of my dictionary discoveries that were not on the homework assignment sheet. But the girls could not contain their glee. They bounded into the kitchen demanding an explanation of the handwritten inscription in fading ink.

My daughter recited the inscription dramatically. "Marie, may this book render assistance to you in the world of literary composition. Love, Ronald. P.S. On the occasion of your 16th birthday."

"What we want to know," said her friend, "is who is this Ronald."

"Sit down," I said. I put two cartons of yogurt and two plastic spoons on the kitchen table for them. My mother would have set out homemade cookies and milk, but times had changed. The maternal instinct for seizing the moment, I suspect, is genetic.

The girls dug into their healthy treat, and I began. "Ronald was my boyfriend when I was 16. He wore white socks to the prom and liked to use big words few people understood. He was quite pompous, as you can see from the inscription. He went on to Yale. I went on to date other young men. And that's all I can tell you about Ronald."

My daughter and her friend shared a look of disappointment. "But that's not the whole story,"

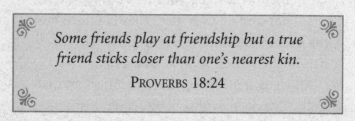

Some friends play at friendship but a true friend sticks closer than one's nearest kin.

PROVERBS 18:24

❖ ◀◯▶ ❖

LOVE AND FRIENDSHIP

Love is like the wild rose-briar,
Friendship like the holly-tree—
The holly is dark when the rose-briar blooms
But which will bloom most constantly?
The wild-rose briar is sweet in the spring,
Its summer blossoms scent the air;
Yet wait till winter comes again
And who will call the wild-briar fair?
Then scorn the silly rose-wreath now
And deck thee with the holly's sheen,
That when December blights thy brow
He may still leave thy garland green.

EMILY BRONTË

❖ ◀◯▶ ❖

I hastened to explain. "On my 16th birthday the florist delivery truck pulled up into the driveway. The flowers were for me! It was my first bouquet. Pink carnations. My mother was right beside me to share my excitement. I ripped open the little card, sighed, and handed it to my mother. She read it out loud: 'Happy Sweet 16, my dearest friend. Love, Bonnie.'"

My daughter turned to her friend. "Would you believe they still send each other flowers every birthday? And talk on the phone for an hour at least once a week?"

"My mother implied it would turn out that way," I said. "She then explained the importance of girlfriends."

My daughter turned back to her friend and said, "When you're an old lady, I will send you pink carnations, too."

Ladies Who Lunch

My friends were eager to see my photos from my vacation to New York City. To my surprise they were less interested in the typical tourist shots of Rockefeller Center, Central Park, a hot dog vendor, and the Statue of Liberty than in my photo of two stylishly dressed ladies having lunch with me in Palm Court at the Plaza Hotel.

"You actually had lunch with those women?" a coworker, Sally, asked during our break at the discount department store where we worked. She could not hide her amazement that I, with my Midwestern simplicity and unsophisticated lifestyle, was acquainted with two women who wore designer clothes and could afford to treat me to a lunch that cost a week's salary.

"I knew them in Georgia," I said. "Tonya and Debbie. We lived in the same trailer park."

"Those women never lived in a trailer. No way!" Sally said. "They look like they have their own jet."

"Fifteen years ago, they lived in a battered trailer with their four kids. Without high school diplomas, they could not find a job. Their husbands had deserted them, and they did not have money to sue for child support. They lived on food stamps and more guts than you can imagine."

Sally sniffed. She was raising two children on her own, so she knew all about guts.

But I knew Sally also needed encouragement, so I continued. "Then Tonya's rattletrap car was repossessed, the day before school started. In it were the children's school clothes, supplies, and shoes that Tonya and Debbie had spent days combing Goodwill and yard sales to get together. That was Tonya's last straw. She cried and cried and told Debbie she may as well put a bullet through her head.

"Debbie told her to put two bullets in the pistol because she would have to go, too. And then who would take care of the kids? That kind of sharp talk from her friend snapped Tonya out of her despair. The two young mothers were up all night, praying together and putting together their plan.

"The next day, they took the bus to a large car dealership and told the manager that they would be quite good at repossessing cars, particularly if the pay was above minimum wage.

"The manager's expression changed from shock to scorn to humor and then to an expression they could not read. 'Okay,' he said. 'I'll give you all we have on a certain deadbeat. You bring in the car, I'll give you $500 and another job.'

"A week later, they brought in the car. The manager could barely talk. Finally, he sputtered out that the car belonged to a murderer who was wanted in three states. The police forces of three states plus the auto dealer's repossession efforts had failed for more than two years, and they had *brought in his car?*

"'And we know where he lives,' Tonya added.

"Debbie was eager to tell him how they'd done it, but Tonya poked her in the ribs. 'Never underestimate the power of prayer and two buddies,' she said. 'Now about that next job?'"

Break time was over, but Sally said she was willing to risk the wrath of our boss to hear the rest of the story.

"It wasn't long before repossessing cars for dealers became routine, not much of a challenge,

---

*Thank you God for my own little
garden of girlfriends—one in the
full bloom of maturity, one in her
last season, and one just
beginning to blossom. One is my
sister in age and shares my mid-
life challenges. One goes before
me and teaches me the grace of
letting go. One reminds me of my
youth and brings back memories
of long-ago joys. Thank you,
God, for girlfriends.*

---

so they started their own business. They are the
only female-owned auto repossession agency in
the state of Georgia. Both got their GEDs and
then went on to college. By living together,
working together, and praying together, they
were able to build a successful business, raise
four kids, and work toward their dreams."

"Why were they in New York?" Sally asked.

I thought she'd never ask. This was the best
part. "Tonya was giving a speech about women
entrepreneurs to classes at Fordham University
in New York City. Debbie was meeting with her
literary agent about the novel she wrote, which

was inspired from their experiences. Also, they had a photo shoot for one of those coffee table books. It's about best friends."

My friend is my counselor with no billable hours,
and when I erupt in rage, she douses the flames.
My friend is my lifeguard when I enter
troubled waters,
and when I melt down in tears,
she wipes them away.
But mostly she's my shady tree
hearing me when I talk,
listening with her heart when I do not.
And often what we do best together is simply be
together anywhere at all.

The Ones That Get Away

My husband, Mark, loves to fish, and so does our next-door neighbor. His wife, Laura, and I have had many long talks about our husbands' friendship. They don't get together to bowl or attend ball games. They fish. Sometimes for an hour or so; sometimes all night. Sometimes from the banks of a nearby river, sometimes in Lake

THE TABLE TURNED

Up! up! my Friend, and quit your books;
Or surely you'll grow double:
Up! up! my Friend, and clear your looks;
Why all this toil and trouble?
…Enough of Science and of Art;
Close up those barren leaves;
Come forth, and bring with you a heart
That watches and receives.

WILLIAM WORDSWORTH

Michigan in their co-owned boat. Sometimes they go together, and sometimes they go fishing alone. Often they bring home fish, and our families have a fish fry. Oddly, they never talk about the ones that get away, which is reputed to be a required portion of the male fishing rite.

One day Laura, an anthropologist, said, "I don't think this fishing has anything to do with the male hunter-gatherer instinct, and as a professional, I need to understand this."

I told her to take off her mortarboard and put on her bonnet. My father was an angler, and my mother had explained long ago why she never complained about the dead squid stench in our garage. My father, she said, worked out his problems with a fishing pole in his hand and sometimes with a fishing buddy beside him. She said she doubted men worked out problems like women did—calling all their friends for empathy and advice. Men just seemed to need to be doing something in times of confusion or crisis, and sometimes they wanted a buddy beside them.

Mom and Dad were pleased I married an angler, although the rest of the world knew Mark as a computer programmer. Mark was surprised that I never complained when he went fishing and that I never asked to go along. Although he doesn't talk about it, I know all about the ones that get away. The time we decided that a job change was right for our family, he went fishing with his friend to make sure the change was right for him. That day he let go of confusion. After watching the sonogram of our first child, he went fishing with my father, and he let go of his fear of becoming a parent. The day he put his father in a nursing home, he fished all night, and he let go of guilt.

Laura promised to observe the fishing expeditions from the lens of a woman, not an anthropologist. At our next fish fry she grinned and said she would offer the table grace. "Thank you, God, for fishing," she said, "and for all the ones that got away. Oh, and please bless this trout and potato salad."

⊶─◇─⊷

Heavenly Father, thank you for my best friend
and bless her abundantly today. Like you,
she knows just by the sound of my voice when
I have something difficult to say. Like you,
she listens patiently and without judgment.
I know that you are just a prayer away,
and I'm grateful that you have answered
a prayer I never thought to pray.
You have given me a friend who is always
just a phone call away.
Amen

⊶─◇─⊷

Chapter Three

Random Acts of Love

*At unexpected moments,
God surprises us with
special blessings through the
kindness of family, friends,
or strangers.*

*N*obody can miss the big, miraculous
blessings that God performs when he
clearly touches hearts and changes lives, but
those blessings come so rarely into our ordinary
days. But most of us have experienced the
unpredictable moments when God sends the
right person or thing at the perfect time. When a
stranger returns a lost wallet, it's an unexpected
blessing. When a check comes in the mail exactly
at the time it's most needed, that's a welcomed
blessing. When an out-of-town friend we
haven't seen in years stops by, we feel so blessed.

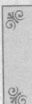

> *I thank my God every time I remember
> you, constantly praying with joy in every
> one of my prayers for all of you.*
>
> PHILIPPIANS 1:3–4

Hundreds of songs and poems remind us of those wonderful and unexpected blessings—the precious little delights that bring us hope and courage to face life's obstacles. We can find God in those moments if we look for him. We can also thank him for the blessings of nature. Something as simple as a crocus pushing up through snowdrifts, a shooting star, or a spectacular sunset. We can even be surprised by the love and kindness of family, friends, and neighbors. A word spoken when we need to hear it or a warm hug; a helping hand during hard times or a gift of true laughter.

Some unexpected blessings can be as large as a life-saving rescue—a stranger pulling trapped children from a burning car or a teen leaping into a lake to help a drowning woman. Other blessings can change our lives by opening doors to a promising new career or a home of our own.

That stranger at the right place at the right time is a blessing. That friend who calls and lifts our spirits on a bad day is a blessing. That child walking past who gives us a dandelion and a trusting smile is a blessing. Watch for those unexpected moments, those blessings at the most surprising times and places—they're gifts from the hand of God.

◆—◆—◀O▶—◆—◆

Dear God,
thank you for tiny flashes of joy
on the darkest days.
Thank you for loving faces
and encouraging words.
Thank you for surprising me
with answered prayers when I least expect it.
Thank you for the wonder and
beauty around me.
Thank you for the peace that
calms my soul.
And thank you for hope
when I have none of my own.
Amen

◆—◆—◀O▶—◆—◆

Discovery

Emmy worried about money. She tried not to, but her job didn't pay well, and she couldn't find anything better. Nevertheless, Mom had always taught her to give back, so she spent at least one night a week volunteering at a Christian coffeehouse.

One Saturday night, she hung her worn, old jacket on a peg in the kitchen, then wrapped herself in an apron and tackled her tasks cheerfully. It was a busy night, but Emmy enjoyed helping out. She scrubbed cups, served homemade cookies to teen customers, and hummed along with the music. Later, she wiped down tables, mopped up spills, and packed away leftover paper cups and napkins. She was tired but felt good about helping youngsters draw closer to God, providing a safe place for kids to go on a

> *I looked for God to send a miracle, something big and dramatic. I wanted to hear his voice like thunder. Instead, he sent a stranger passing on the sidewalk who smiled, and I heard God whisper a love song to my heart.*

weekend. When she was done, she removed her apron and grabbed her jacket from its hook.

Automatically, she reached inside the pocket, where she usually kept what few dollars she had. Her stomach dropped. There were no dollar bills there. Had she been robbed while serving God?

No, wait, she remembered spending those dollars earlier in the day. No theft after all. But as her fingers slid deeper into the pocket, she touched something. Something crisp and new. She tugged it out and stared. She counted three neatly folded fifty-dollar bills. Her stomach fluttered, and she felt stunned.

She asked her coworkers, but nobody would admit putting anything inside her pocket. One friend hugged her and said, "Listen, Em, if God wants to surprise you with a gift, don't ask a lot of questions. Just take it and tell him thanks!"

Grateful tears slid down Emmy's cheeks as she hugged her friend back and thanked God in her heart. It didn't matter who had placed the cash in her pocket. Emmy knew it was a blessing sent straight from God!

UNEXPECTED MOMENTS

Lord, we find you in unexpected moments.
In shared laughter between a mom and
her rebellious teen.
In a quick hug from a loving friend.
In a kind word from a total stranger.
In a gentle touch from a weary spouse.
In a TV commercial that makes us giggle.
In a sunset that stirs hearts and spirits.
In all the small and precious times when we
least expect to see you and so gladly welcome
your constant care and wonderful blessings.

Hockey Dreaming

Alex wanted to play hockey. It was his dream, and he wanted it with his whole heart. But as Mom pointed out on a daily basis, they didn't have money for expensive hockey gear—helmet, skates, shoulder pads, shin guards, and so on. Mom had seen the prices in Alex's hockey catalogs. She knew even bargain gear would add up to hundreds of dollars.

"We just don't have the money, hon, you know that."

Just one simple act of kindness might make someone's day.

Alex didn't argue. He understood. Mom and Dad worked hard. Prices were high. Bills were higher. But, oh, how he yearned to play hockey, to test his strength, and to feel the weight of a hockey stick in his hands. Playing street hockey wasn't the same. He wanted to be out on the ice, but there was no way. Might as well expect money to fall from the sky.

Alex got a part-time job, hoping to earn the cash himself, but it would take years to earn what he needed. Still he dreamed. He watched games on TV, imagining himself out there on the ice. He read hockey books and magazines. And when a team started up in his town, Uncle Luke took him to a bunch of games. Alex loved it. He loved being so cold that he couldn't feel his fingers or toes. He loved risking life and limb every time a puck smacked into the stands. He loved cheering when his team scored.

Then one day, Uncle Luke stopped by early before the game. "Listen," he told Alex, "it seems to me you'd make a great hockey player. You love the game. So, if you're interested, I thought I might buy you some equipment to get you started. What do you think?"

Alex thought he might explode. He couldn't find words. Excitement bubbled inside him, and he wanted to hug Uncle Luke, except Alex was way too old for hugging.

"Yeah, uh, sure," he managed. "That would be great."

They shopped for gear. Alex loved every moment. Trying on shoulder pads felt like heaven. Hefting a hockey stick in both gloved hands made his heart leap. Looking at himself in a mirror once he was in his gear made Alex feel as if he owned the world.

Some day he might play on a pro team. Some day he hoped to win trophies. Some day he might even play on a team that wins the Stanley Cup. And Uncle Luke's blessing started it all!

* * *

Dear Lord, today my daughter gave me a flower for no reason—just because she thought of me. She asked me why I was crying, and I couldn't explain. In that moment, I thought my heart would burst with love! Thank you for giving her to me.

* * *

Unexpected Friendships

I can't even remember why I decided to try going to the young mothers' church group. Maybe I wanted to get out of the house. Having a young child at home can be exhausting. There were days when I craved adult contact—besides the letter carrier, that is. My daughter was a delight, and I loved her completely. But some-times I would go stir crazy and need to be out among older people.

One major plus about this group was the free child care. I could get out, be among other adults, and be sure my daughter had fun, too. It was wonderful, restful, and fun. The other women were mostly strangers, but we got along okay. After that first meeting, I went to collect my daughter. The other women all milled around gathering up their youngsters, too. We smiled at one another, then slipped back into the world of focusing on our little ones.

My daughter erupted from the room—she never walked if she could run—for she had found herself a friend. The two little girls hit it off perfectly. They'd been together for one morning, and they were instant almost-sisters.

They were not interested in going home. They wanted to be together.

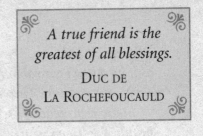

A true friend is the greatest of all blessings.

DUC DE
LA ROCHEFOUCAULD

The other mom and I were swept along with the girls. We wound up setting up times to get together so the girls could see each other again. The girls, heads close, giggling, whispering, having a fine time, loved the idea of visiting each other's home. So we two moms agreed. We switched back and forth, one time at our house, next time at theirs. We brought food and shared lunch. We let the girls do crafts, which they both adored—both were highly creative.

The girls seemed closer than siblings—they argued less. Both girls loved reading and playing with their dolls. They could spend hours and still beg for more. The other mom and I enjoyed seeing them have so much fun. Of course, being thrown together while our girls played, we started getting to know each other, too.

I can't say when it happened. I don't know at what moment we stopped being the mothers of two girls who loved being together and became friends. Who can say just when the relationship

*I hear a lot of people ask the question
"Where is God?" as if he is hiding from us,
as if he doesn't care about us. I wonder why
they don't see him. They just aren't looking
in the right places. I see him standing
behind the friend who offers me a ride on a
stormy day. I see him nudging the neighbor
who calls to check to see if I'm doing okay.
I see him in a dozen surprising places.*

shifted. But after a while, we were talking on the phone, making our own plans.

Years passed. The girls drifted apart, as sometimes childhood friendships do. But we two moms had forged something so strong and solid between us; we had become so close that we talked almost daily. We knew each other's likes and dislikes, each other's hopes and dreams. We shared prayer requests and celebrated each other's joys. We shared maternity clothes, recipes, and favorite books.

Our friendship began as a by-product of our daughters' friendship, but it has become an amazing, precious, and unexpected blessing. One of God's random acts of love.

·❖·❮O❯·❖·

Almighty God, maker of the universe, you set the world in motion. You made the sun, moon, and stars. You created all living things. Yet you find time to give us each small, wonderful, and unexpected blessings where we wouldn't think to look for them.

·❖·❮O❯·❖·

Dirty Dishes

Laura felt more embarrassed than ever before in her life. She'd been so busy lately, so swamped meeting class deadlines and keeping up with her part-time job. Her apartment had gotten completely out of control. Somehow she hadn't realized how bad it was until her friend from work, Nila, stopped by to visit.

Dishes stacked beside the sink threatened to topple over. Pots and pans, most only half rinsed, filled the sink to the top. Empty food packages crammed the overflowing garbage can, and bits of cereal had tumbled onto the floor and hardened there. The tabletop was stained and speckled with yucky stuff. Laura couldn't believe she'd let it get this bad. The smell alone was awful.

It was such a small apartment that you could see the bedroom from the front door. Clothes covered the floor, bed, and chair. Toiletries lay jumbled around on every surface. Drying towels draped from chair backs and the foot of the bed. Dirty laundry heaped in several baskets.

Laura felt her face blush fiery red.

"Oh, I'm so sorry," she mumbled to her friend. "I haven't had time to breathe lately. If I'd known you were coming, I'd have cleaned up." She spread her hands in helplessness. Looking at her home as her friend must see it, she thought it would take a bulldozer and a dozen hard-hat workers to tackle this mess.

What would Nila think of her?

Nila grinned suddenly. "Don't worry. I went to school once myself. I know what a rough schedule it is keeping up with both class and work. I'll tell you what, I was going to invite you out for a walk to get some exercise. Why don't we tackle your apartment instead. That should be enough exercise for anybody." As she spoke, she rummaged for dish towels and scrubbing sponges.

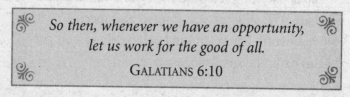

So then, whenever we have an opportunity, let us work for the good of all.

GALATIANS 6:10

The most wonderful moments of any day are those unexpected blessings—a baby's laughter, a movie that makes you cry, a hug when you need one most, a friend calling just to say hi, or someone saying, "You're beautiful."

Still feeling ashamed of the mess her apartment had become, Laura wanted to argue. But Nila seemed cheerful and calm and determined to help, as if this wasn't the worst disaster she'd ever seen. Nila had rolled up her shirtsleeves and was scraping old food from dishes, slipping them into a sinkful of water to soak.

"You don't have to do this," Laura tried to argue. "I'm just so embarrassed."

"Don't be," Nila told her. "If we could sneak inside people's homes when they least expect us, I suspect we'd find plenty of unwashed dishes and piled-up laundry. You're not alone. There are days my place makes yours look sparkling clean. So, come on, let's go. Then I'll treat for ice cream as a reward. We'll deserve it!"

Side by side they tackled the mess and finished up in far less time than it would have taken Laura alone. When they were done, Laura stood staring. The place looked wonderful and smelled much, much better. Nila had found some room freshener and lemon-scented cleanser, which also perfumed the air.

"Okay," Nila said, packing away the cleaning supplies and dish towels, "let's go have that treat. And listen, don't hesitate to ask if you want company cleaning again some time. Doing it together makes it much easier."

Laura nodded and felt a burst of deep gratitude. Thank God for friends who didn't mind helping out with the nastiest, messiest kitchen in recorded history!

Supermarket Friends

I don't know what to call them except supermarket friends. When I stop by the store each morning to get fresh donuts for my aging mom's breakfast, they're there, working. We chat, complain about the weather, brag about our kids' latest achievements, compliment each other on earrings or outfits. We don't go to one another's homes or eat out together. Sometimes we don't even know one another's last names.

But we're friends anyway in that particular place and time. There've been times we've told

> *Oh, Lord, I need your help with so many problems and worries. I can't cope on my own. I sometimes feel so overwhelmed. Then, just when I need help the most, you send someone to be there for me. Thank you, Lord.*

personal things, problems we're facing or worries about our kids. We've prayed for each other and shared our joy and relief when prayers have been answered.

So I don't know what else to call them except my supermarket friends. When my mom suddenly fell very ill, I found myself in a hospital corridor, trembling, deeply shaken, tears running down my face. The doctor had just told me my mom would probably die, perhaps within an hour. It hit me hard, and I felt lost, not knowing what to do or how to handle it. It was hard to make calls to my family—my voice shook so badly, and I couldn't remember the most familiar phone numbers.

Suddenly there in the hallway stood one of my supermarket friends. She just happened to be there that day. The story poured from me. I was so glad, so thankful to see a familiar face. She listened and cared, her eyes full of sympathy. She

STANDING IN LINE

Waiting for the doors to open,
eager for a bargain
outside the new store,
one woman looks so weary,
her hair already drooping
before 9:00 A.M., and the
children fussing.
A stranger, watching, smiles
and asks, "Is it okay?"
and offers suckers.
The children enjoy their treats.
Their mom looks five years
younger and truly
blessed.

hugged me and offered words of comfort and courage, though I don't recall just what she said. It was enough. Her kindness got me through those first unbearable moments of hearing I might lose my mom.

I made my calls, and I decided what treatment the doctors should provide for my mom. She astounded the doctors and nurses by pulling out of the coma. After six weeks in the hospital, she recovered enough to come back home.

When I went back to the store the first morning she felt well enough for her normal breakfast of fresh donuts, there were my supermarket friends, asking about her health and offering kindness.

"How's your mom doing?" they still ask when I go in for donuts each morning. They genuinely care. And I am forever grateful that God sent me these amazing friends.

Quietly Being There

Jenny's husband died suddenly on a bright Tuesday afternoon. No warning. No signs or symptoms. No time for saying good-bye. It seemed to Jenny that one instant he was fine, the same as always, and the next he was simply gone. She could hardly comprehend what had happened. She felt as if this were all some terrible mistake, that Andy would walk through the door any minute—that none of it had happened after all.

Somebody told her best friend Judith that it was a sort of protective shock—that it would help her get through what needed to be done. But Jenny felt like a zombie. She walked,

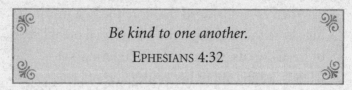

Be kind to one another.
EPHESIANS 4:32

talked, made decisions when she had to, and pretty much seemed to be there. But she wasn't really. In her mind she relived days she and Andy had shared, times they'd laughed together, better times.

She moved through the funeral as if she were not aware of anything at all. Judith decided that was good for now. So Jenny never even noticed that Judith handled dozens of situations that arose and settled all sorts of problems and questions. Jenny wasn't aware when her next-door neighbor stopped by, gathered up the girls, and took them home with her. She hardly noticed when the rest of the neighbors came in to straighten up her house or take in her relatives who'd come for the funeral.

Members of her church showed up with casseroles and salads to fill her refrigerator. Jenny hardly noticed anything she ate anyway, but they knew she needed good food to help keep her going. Her daughters came home to change clothes and get their school books and papers, but the neighbor pretty much kept the girls at her home, making sure they got to school and ate good lunches.

The man who lived on the other side of Jenny's house mowed her grass when he did his own. Judith moved in to keep an eye on Jenny who still went through her days as if she were only half aware of where she was. Judith kept up with dirty laundry and checked on the girls to be sure they had everything they needed.

At school, the teachers gently helped the girls through each day, simply by being kind, by caring, by listening when the girls needed to talk. The guidance counselor called them down for quiet sessions once a week to be sure they were doing okay. The girls spent a few hours each day at home with their mom, and she hugged them, loved them, and helped a little with their homework.

Distant friends sent letters and cards. One friend even sent a book on the stages of grief, and Jenny put the book aside, thinking maybe someday she'd read it. Judith kept the cards and letters, waiting until Jenny felt ready to deal with them.

Some days Jenny cried a lot. Some days she worked hard to keep busy. Other days she gathered all her strength and told Judith what to give away and what to keep among Andy's things. Judith was almost always there, standing by.

And finally one day, Jenny looked around and noticed all that had been done, quietly and kindly around her. She noticed the neatly mowed grass and the casseroles that still appeared in the fridge. She saw that her daughters were getting rides to school every day and good lunches. She realized that somebody had done laundry and washed dishes.

"Who did all this?" she asked Judith.

"People who care," Judith told her.

Then they cried together for awhile, and at last, Jenny began to mend.

Dear Lord, thank you for the many blessings you have poured into my life—both the big and the small things that people have done for me. These blessings and these people are all truly wonderful. They have taught me how to embrace your love and how to express your love to others. Please continue to bring such loving people into my life—as well as the people you want me to love. Amen

Chapter Four

There's No Place Like Home

We can thank God for our homes, communities, and nation, which sustain us and give us strength.

Sometimes, like what Dorothy experienced in *The Wizard of Oz*, our experiences whirl us off into distant and unusual places. We might find ourselves far from our own familiar worlds. Yet, so often we feel the pull of home. We yearn for the places we know best and the people left behind.

Like Dorothy, we usually discover after all our adventures that "There's no place like home." Home is where we go for rest and safety, where we find peace and contentment. Home can be a two-story farmhouse or a suburban ranch-style house, a mansion, or a mobile trailer. The building itself can be anything, but what pulls us back is something more—a sense of roots and belonging.

In a larger sense, home can be the town or city where we live, the neighborhood where we grew up, or the church where we've always worshiped and recognize every face. But home can also be our nation, where we cherish our many precious freedoms.

Perhaps we don't always realize how much home means to us. Only when we're far away, like Dorothy was in Oz, do we become more fully aware of how much we value our homes, the places where we've left our hearts. So it's a joy and delight to recognize how blessed we are to have homes, neighborhoods, communities, churches, and a nation we can thank God for giving us.

> *It is only when we are far from home that we realize how precious is the home God has given us. For when we leave home, something of our hearts is left behind to call us ever back again.*

Welcome Home

He was glad to be home. You could tell just by looking at him. But he was weary, too. Seeing him in his uniform, clearly military and definitely home on leave, he looked as if he'd seen much that was difficult, much that demanded a lot of him. On the plane, he leaned his head back and dozed, as if he hadn't had enough rest in a very long time.

So young. Just a boy in a way, yet a boy who had become a man while serving his country. How long had he been away? How far from home? You couldn't help but wonder what his story was, what he'd experienced. He kept his military discipline, shoulders squared and chin steady, a man who'd been trained well.

> *Oh, Lord, on stormy nights, I think of you and all you've given us. Shelter from the wind and rain and fierce bolts of lightning. Safety and protection. Homes, neighbors, communities, churches, and a nation where we are free to be ourselves, where we are free to worship, and where we are free to count our many and wonderful blessings.*

＊＊━◁○▷━＊＊

*Dear Lord, when my family is far from home,
keep them safe. Please watch over them while we
are apart, and remind them home is always here
to welcome them when they return. Please bless
everyone who is far from home today, and bring
them all safely back again. Amen*

＊＊━◁○▷━＊＊

Then there was the homecoming. You could
see his step quicken on the walk from the plane.
The burden weighing down his body a few minutes earlier lifted and, at least for now, was gone.
He'd served his country and stood up for what
he believed. But now he was on home ground.
As he passed by, he gazed on familiar objects.

His stride quickened even more. Just around
the next corner. Just up ahead. In the waiting,
watching crowd, people craned their necks looking for their friends and family members depart-
ing the plane. You could tell instantly which ones
were his. A young woman lifted a toddler high to
see over the heads around them.

"Here's Daddy," she told the child. Beside
her the older couple had to be his parents, the
woman with tears on her cheeks, the man fighting to hold back the emotion. A younger brother
stood with them, stepping forward to meet him.

He walked faster, passing through the mob around him with eyes only for them. They cut through the crowd to meet him as if there were no other people in the busy airport. Then they were with him, pushing in on all sides. Who to hug first? Mom with one arm, wife and baby with the other. A hand stretched out to shake with Dad. The younger brother patting his shoulder, and all of them with watery eyes.

Everyone talked at once, telling him they'd missed him, saying how proud they were of him, and asking if he'd had a good flight. They hugged and hugged some more. They were jostled from all sides but were totally unaware of anyone else around them.

The rest of us passed slowly by, soaking it up, feeling our own hearts lifted with all that joy and love, feeling our own eyes tearing along with them. And as we went quietly past them, we could hear his mother telling him, "God has answered my prayers. Thank God, you're home."

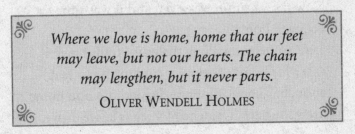

Where we love is home, home that our feet may leave, but not our hearts. The chain may lengthen, but it never parts.

OLIVER WENDELL HOLMES

HOME PLACE

Crumbling brick and peeling paint,
the place is old, so very old,
and so in need of repair.
Rotting floors and the smell of mold,
a place left alone too long,
a place empty and almost forgotten.
Still, once it was home for someone
and treasured, a safe place,
a welcoming place—a home place,
a place of love, joy, hope—a blessed place.

Home Again

We'd been traveling all day, driving for hours on end. Our vacation had been lovely. We'd enjoyed every second. Swimming in the ocean. Touring theme parks. Relaxing on the beach. Walking until our feet ached but happy anyway. Now the vacation was over, and it was time to get back home.

At some point along the way, I found myself eager for home. The miles couldn't go by fast enough. The vacation was behind me, and home drew me back. I watched for signs as we drove, counting how many miles to go, how many hours before we'd see familiar sights and landmarks. There were still many miles to go, and the sky was becoming dark.

"Should we stop somewhere for the night?" my husband asked. I found myself reluctant to pause on the homeward journey. I wanted to push on and reach home as soon as possible.

I shook my head. "Why don't we keep going. We're almost there."

"Okay," he agreed. We were tired, but I think home called to us both.

My heart lifted when we saw signs for cities not far from our own. Then we spotted familiar places—the mall three towns over, the airport, the turnoff for our town. With each familiar place, my spirit quickened. Almost home, soon now, soon.

Each place we passed felt so good and comforting. The kids' schools, the car dealership where we bought our station wagon, the church where we spent so much of our time. Then our own driveway and front door. Noisily we tumbled from the car, a chaos of grabbing suitcases and bags full of souvenirs. The next few minutes we carried stuff back and forth, dumping them on the living room floor.

It was after dark, and we were all exhausted from the long trip. The kids went willingly to bed. We checked the stack of mail waiting for us and made sure the doors were locked and everything was in order.

"Don't worry about unpacking tonight," my husband said, yawning, stretching, clearly tired from the long day in the car. As he went off to bed, I promised to be right along behind him.

But I had a few things to do first. Quietly I walked the house from end to end. I checked the kids who'd fallen asleep practically on their feet, flopping into bed still in their clothes. I slipped off their shoes and tucked them in. I prowled the empty rooms, which felt as if nobody had been there in months rather than days.

It was as if I had to reclaim my territory. I straightened throw pillows on the sofa and tidied a wobbly pile of magazines. I checked the fridge and started a list of groceries we'd need the next day. I hung fresh towels on the bathroom racks.

And the whole time, what went through my mind was enormous gratitude to God for this place—my home—for each room and piece of furniture, for each photo on the wall and each moment spent there. Being away, even for a few days, somehow made me love it more, this place that was my home. In my heart I thanked God for our home, for our lovely neighborhood, and for all the fine people who lived there.

Vacations were great, but getting home again was the finest blessing of all.

HOMESICKNESS

Can anyone explain it?
Can anyone make it clear?
Why we miss it so,
why we yearn for the
place we call home?
Why it beckons to us whether
we are five miles away
or five hundred?
Why no matter how far
we travel or
how long we're gone,
home draws us, tugs us,
pulls us back again
with yearning, hungry,
thankful hearts?

Small Town Pride

I grew up in a small town—a clean, quiet, and lovely place. Everybody knew everybody else. We all knew who was related and how. We knew who worked at what job. We knew what kind of car everyone in town drove. In fact, we could drive past a grocery store parking lot, check the cars there, and know who was inside shopping.

There was plenty of grass, broad lawns, and country roads. Our house was a mile from town, an easy walk in nice weather. Fields surrounded our home. In harvest time we picked leftovers from the fields: sweet potatoes, tomatoes, and strawberries. Talk about fresh produce—nobody could have it any fresher than picking it ourselves.

I had a few pet chickens, a dog, two cats, and occasionally turtles or snakes that wandered into the yard. I rode a bus to school and enjoyed visiting the horses just down the road. Life was slow

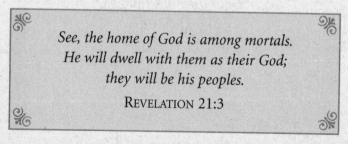

*See, the home of God is among mortals.
He will dwell with them as their God;
they will be his peoples.*

REVELATION 21:3

and sweet there in that town. We went to movies on Friday nights and walked Main Street in groups, joking and laughing. We split ice cream sodas or hot fudge sundaes. We always went to

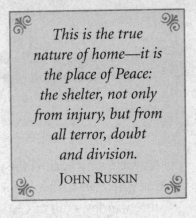

This is the true nature of home—it is the place of Peace: the shelter, not only from injury, but from all terror, doubt and division.

JOHN RUSKIN

church and out for brunch at the diner afterward.

And holidays, oh, the holidays were best of all. Halloween meant contests where every shop window held a poster painted by the school kids. We also piled into the back of pickup trucks to go door-to-door for treats, and we wore costumes our moms made at home on their sewing machines. And sometimes we played tricks, which weren't nasty, and we'd sing or dance or recite poetry.

Thanksgiving meant food and more food. Moms working from early morning, fixing turkey and pies, dressing and gravy. We'd all pitch in some, but there were the parades on TV to watch, too.

The competition and fun of Christmas decorations, houses so lit up we could see them miles

> *Let every person be subject to the governing authorities; for there is no authority except from God, and those authorities that exist have been instituted by God.*
>
> ROMANS 13:1

away, glowing against the night sky. The town tree where we gathered for the decorating. The store windows full of Christmas gift ideas.

I loved all the holidays and all the fun. But most of all I loved Christmas when we celebrated the birth of Jesus. Those were joyful times of togetherness for the whole town. That was also true for the Fourth of July. Everybody turned out for the parades down Main Street. I remember learning how to do a quick shuffle of feet to get back in step with my marching Girl Scout troop. Everybody who had ever served in the military marched, wearing as much of the uniform that still fit, especially the hats.

Dear God, I pray for my country—that it will truly be a home to all who seek you and hope to worship you in freedom. Amen

We'd march or watch the marching. We'd hear the high school band blaring out patriotic songs. We'd gather at the memorial statues and read the names of those who had given their lives for their country. We'd see flags proudly flying from porches and windowsills, front yard poles, and garden planters. We'd wear red, white, and blue and sometimes tiny flag pins on our collars.

We wore red paper poppies in remembrance of veterans, and we gathered to hear the war stories shared at the town picnic. Then there'd be hot dogs and soft drinks. And of course there would be fireworks, where we'd sit on blankets late into the night and ohhh and ahhh over the beauty of the displays. Then at last we'd go home again,

Our flag has flown through good times and bad, at half-staff for our losses and high for our celebrations. Why is our flag so important to us? Because it represents all that we are, all that makes us who we are. The flag unites us, no matter what we do or where we find ourselves. Whatever our background, whatever we believe, the flag brings us together as one people, one nation—the flag represents all that is home for us and all that we can be thankful for!

feeling thankful to God for our town and for
our nation.

That's what home means to me—that small
town with its huge celebrations and understanding how richly blessed we are to be here—in the
land of the free, in the land God has given us.

Moving

Lisa bent over cardboard boxes, unloading dishes
and pots until her back screamed for mercy.
Moving was not fun. At least not when you did it
often. Sitting on one full, closed box to rest, Lisa
added it up. They'd been married slightly more
than a year, she and James, and in that time they
must have moved five times. "Or was it six, Lord?"

From their wedding trip, they'd come home to
a tiny apartment with no air conditioning and
hardly any space to walk past each other in the
tiny hallway. Lisa hadn't minded. It was theirs,
and she'd planned to make it into a home for
them. Then James came home one day, excited
about an offer his boss had made.

"We can live in their house while they're out
of the country," he explained. "It's huge and gor-

geous. You'll love it, Lis. All we have to do is water the plants, feed the dogs, and it's ours for free! Can you believe what God has opened up for us?"

"Sounds interesting," Lisa told her new husband, feeling less than enthusiastic but not wanting to spoil his excitement.

"You will absolutely love this place. It's what we might have for our own someday. Wait and see; you'll be crazy about it." Then James was off to make plans for the move.

Of course, things became complicated. Because the apartment lease expired three weeks before his boss left, James and Lisa moved in briefly with his brother. Lisa tried not to mind. Living out of boxes for three weeks wasn't the end of the world. But it wasn't what she'd imagined for her first year of marriage either.

Moving into the boss's house took plenty of hard work, but the place was everything James

* · ◆ · ◄〇►· ◆ ·

Dear Lord, such a hectic day, rushing here and there with so much to do. It's so good to get home, to slip off my shoes, and to feel the peace of being in this place you've provided—this place of warmth and welcome.

· ◆ · ◄〇►· ◆ ·

said it was. But, of course, things became complicated again. The boss ran into some problems during his trip and had to cut it short. That meant Lisa and James had to repack all their belongings much sooner than expected.

Since they couldn't find a new apartment quickly enough, it was back in with James's brother, who was being really nice about the whole thing.

Now, in her new apartment, Lisa was unpacking yet again. She couldn't help asking God whether they'd stay long enough to get everything unpacked this time. They'd moved time after time, and she felt weary of it.

"Is this it?" she asked her new husband. "Will we be able to settle down here for awhile?" She held her breath, waiting. Living out of boxes and never having a place to call home was not her plan for their life as husband and wife.

"Sure, Lis," James told her. "Well, unless something better comes along. We could use a bigger place, and I'm still watching for a house for us. One of those fixer-upper types. We'd have fun painting and repairing it."

"But," Lisa protested, "I'm so tired of moving, of never getting really settled, of never having a home of our own." She felt close to tears.

James looked up, his eyes full of surprise. "But, Lis, everywhere we've been has been home for us. As long as we're together, God will take care of us. Wherever you are, that's home for me."

Lisa felt a rush of love for her husband so strong that she thought she might burst with it. And it hit her for the first time. Home wasn't a particular place. Home was how you felt being with the people you cared most about. With a huge hug for her new husband, Lisa lifted her heart in gratitude to God that she and James could be together, wherever their home might be.

Good Neighbors

Sam glanced out the front window and frowned slightly. "Have you seen Mrs. Parrish lately?" he asked his wife, Dawn.

Looking up from a stack of newspapers she was gathering to recycle, Dawn shook her head. "No, actually, I don't remember seeing her yesterday or today."

"That's not right," Sam said, still staring out at their neighbor's house. "She's always in and out, walking the dog, watering her flowers. Usually we see her at least two or three times a day."

Dawn shrugged. "Maybe she went to visit somebody."

"No," Sam argued. "Remember, she told us once she has no family left, that she hates to travel, and that she wouldn't have anybody to take care of her dog if she went away."

"Yeah, I guess you're right. So, what do we do?"

He watched for a few more minutes and saw the letter carrier coming down the block. Sam walked out to meet him. When Sam asked, the letter carrier mentioned he'd been wondering about it too.

"She hadn't gotten her mail yesterday from the day before. I mean, we don't hit the panic button for one day, but if she hasn't gotten it by today, then I might need to call somebody. That isn't like her. She's usually right there at the door waiting for me, eager for her mail, though it's often just ads."

"Let's take a look," offered Sam. There was all their neighbor's mail piled up in her box.

"This is all of it," the letter carrier said. "She hasn't gotten it for two days."

That was enough for Sam. Standing on Mrs. Parrish's front step, he started banging on the

> *I was born near the sea, and I hear it singing deep inside of me. I may live hundreds of miles away, but in my heart it's never far. Whenever I can, I go there to walk the beach and draw salty air into my lungs and feel sand between my toes, soaking something vast and awesome I find only beside the sea. It's in my blood, the sea. It's home to me and always will be. And it speaks to me of God—of his power. And I am always blessed there.*

door and ringing the doorbell. He heard her dog's frantic yapping but that was all. Together he and the letter carrier walked around the house, tapping on windows, listening for any unusual sounds.

"Does anybody have a key?" asked the letter carrier. Sam didn't think so, but he went door to door among the other nearby neighbors to ask. Nobody had a key. Nobody had seen Mrs. Parrish for two days. Everybody expressed concern. Pretty soon, the neighborhood was gathered on the sidewalk outside her house discussing the situation.

"I say we pry open a window and go in," offered one neighbor.

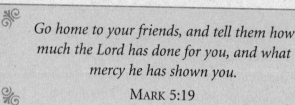

Go home to your friends, and tell them how much the Lord has done for you, and what mercy he has shown you.

MARK 5:19

"Doesn't she have anybody we can call? Family or anything?" asked another, but Sam shook his head.

"Guess it's up to us," Sam finally said. "I think we should dial 911, get the fire department and police out here. They can go in and check whether she's okay." The others nodded in agreement, and one immediately used a cell phone to call for help.

In no time at all, an ambulance arrived, followed closely by the police and the fire department. After some discussion and confirmation that no one had seen Mrs. Parrish in two days, the rescuers agreed to enter the house. While they found a window they could pry open, everyone stood in clumps talking and waiting.

Next thing they knew, the paramedics were coming in and out of the front door. "We found her inside," one of them told the waiting neighbors. "She'll be alright, but she had a bad fall and couldn't call for help. Good thing you people thought to get help for her."

Then they were carrying Mrs. Parrish out to the ambulance. Sam stepped forward, and she reached for his hand.

In a weak voice, his neighbor said, "I'm so glad there was somebody to care. Thank God for good neighbors. Take care of my doggie, please."

"Sure thing," Sam agreed, squeezing her hand gently as she was wheeled past.

"I'll be home soon," she whispered to no one in particular.

Lord God, please bless our home. Bless each room and all within its walls. May we remember to be thankful for all we have—food and light, heat and shelter. May we appreciate the rich and endless blessings we enjoy in this wonderful nation of ours. And may we always reach out to others to share what we have. Thank you, Lord, for our daily blessings.
Amen

Chapter Five

The Healing Power of Nature

The Creator has adorned this world with his many splendors, and in our enjoyment of those splendors, many of our ills are relieved.

The psalmist David says the Lord leads us beside still waters and restores our soul. What a wonderful observation this poet-king shares with us! Nature, whether in a flowerpot or acres of rain forest or a flowing stream, has spoken to poets, saints, and sages through the centuries. But nature also speaks to each one of us if we will only listen as David did.

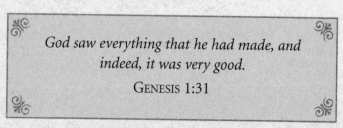

God saw everything that he had made, and indeed, it was very good.

GENESIS 1:31

Living in harmony with nature's seasons awakens us to spring's renewal, fall's cozy slowness, winter's savory rest, and summer's exuberance. Thus we are reminded to honor each season's energies for the wisdom they hold.

When we take the time to look at the world around us and see the handiwork of God, nature can soothe our spirit and heal our heart. It is at such times that we should worship the Lord with our deep gratitude for what he has given each one of us.

Heavenly Father, thank you for the showers that nourish the flowers and the trees. Thank you for the lofty mountains and the roaring seas. Thank you for the birds and the creatures in the oceans, and thank you for our furry friends. You have called us to be responsible guardians of this world. Help us be good stewards of all that you have made for us to enjoy.

My Mother's Secret Garden

My mother didn't exactly have a green thumb; we called it a wild one, and we never knew from one season to the next what would be growing or failing to thrive in her garden. Usually only rain watered it, and often it was weedy. "A mom," she would say, "with six kids doesn't have time to be a gardener. But a mom with six kids needs a garden."

My mother's garden always had a place for sitting. I recall a splintery straight-back wooden chair that she finally replaced with a gracefully curved cement bench. An upended metal garbage can lid on a stump served as a birdbath until the Christmas we presented her with a real one from the landscape department of a discount store. From our picnics by the river, she had collected flat rocks and stones over the years to build a path from our back door to her garden.

She did not care if we played in her garden and never behaved as though it were anything more than a part of our backyard. Fruit-drink spills on her bench were never mentioned;

*Cultivate the garden of your heart, and
watch love bloom!*

plants were uprooted for science projects. Soccer
balls smashed fragile stalks. We made daisy
chains from summer's bounty, and we tried to
sell them door-to-door. Mom was the only person who bought one.

I know she visited her garden in the morning.
Sometimes I would see her wipe the dew from
her bare feet on the rug by the back door before
she thought anyone had risen. Every time I saw
her come in from the garden, she would be
humming the same tune. I never thought to ask
her what she was humming. The music was just
a part of mom in the morning.

Mother's garden is tidy now, just a well-
tended rosebush. It wasn't until her funeral that
we realized why she always had a garden and
always hummed the same tune in the morning.
The hymn she requested for her funeral was
titled "In the Garden." We instantly recognized
the tune. The lyrics [on the next page] explained
why our mother always had a garden and how a
mother who raised six children alone was able to
begin every day with a song that spoke of her
closeness to God.

IN THE GARDEN

I come to the garden alone
While the dew is still on the roses
And the voice I hear
Falling on my ear
The Son of God discloses.
And he walks with me
And he talks with me
And he tells me I am his own
And the joy we share
As we tarry there
None other has ever known.

C. AUSTIN MILES

The Holiest of Holidays

I have always loved Christmas Eve, even better than Christmas, because it is a day of expectation of the hope and joy God gave to us on earth. Of course, as a child, the expectation had a great deal to do with the festively wrapped presents under the tree and the other presents in my grandparents' car. As a mother, the expectation was of my children's joy, but I always took a few minutes after they were asleep and Santa had made his deliveries to ponder the mysteries of love and faith.

Wanting Christmas Eve to be as special for my children, I always let them unwrap one gift before they went to bed—right after I read them the story of Christ's birth. First there were board books they would chew on, then picture books, and finally the story right from our family Bible.

I knew my first Christmas as an "empty nester" would be difficult. Distance and my work kept me from my children that holiday. Thanks to a grant, I was living on an island 30 miles out to sea doing wildlife research that could not be interrupted. Nevertheless, I was intentional about filling Christmas Day with activities: church, dinner with friends, and two videos that had become a family tradition.

But on Christmas Eve I was pensive, perhaps a bit depressed. I had no one to share this special day with, and the only activity on the island was Midnight Mass at the island's little church. I gave up trying to work on my research project and

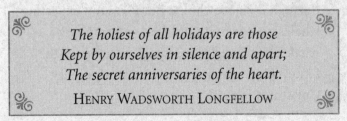

The holiest of all holidays are those
Kept by ourselves in silence and apart;
The secret anniversaries of the heart.
HENRY WADSWORTH LONGFELLOW

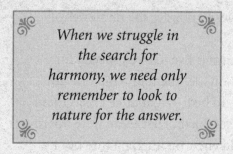

> *When we struggle in the search for harmony, we need only remember to look to nature for the answer.*

jumped into my Jeep. It had special tires for driving on sand, and I knew I could count on the roar of the surf to speak to me of God's majesty.

I drove down the deserted beach for a few miles to the island's point. I honked the horn. Seals barked back. They always made me laugh. But I wasn't laughing that day. I got out of the Jeep and walked along the shore looking down for treasures: A rare shell? An ancient gold coin? No, just the usual seaweed, shell fragments, and Styrofoam.

I looked out to sea again expecting to see my aching emptiness reflected there. I saw steam. Was there a little volcano under the sea so close to shore? Three volcanoes? Ten? If I had been expecting to see it, I would have known immediately that I was looking at whales spouting water through their blowholes. But I was not expecting whales, so it wasn't until I saw a humpback whale breech and plunge back into the sea that I knew God was giving me an extraordinary Christmas Eve gift.

Dear God, thank you for the daisies I saw on my drive to work today, for the cattails around the pond, and the red-winged blackbirds that flew away. Thank you for memories of the days I walked barefoot through your beauty, picking flowers and chasing whistling birds. And thank you for the thought you just put into my head that I can stop the car, kick off my shoes, and walk through your beauty again today on my way home from work. Yes, Lord, tonight supper can wait.

Rosemary for Remembrance

When I was eight years old, my Aunt Esther took me to The Cloisters, which is a medieval museum on the banks of the Hudson River in New York. It was not her first visit, for one of her hobbies was painting. From oil painting to piano to travels to exotic places, she delved deeply into her interests. On the drive to The Cloisters, she told me about the Middle Ages, introducing me to castles, knights and their ladies, the Black Plague, the Inquisition, and writers, such as Chaucer, whom I would later study in high school.

Such information could be boring to an eight-year-old, but she was a first-grade teacher, and she knew how to talk to children in a way that engaged them and made them feel grown-up. I particularly liked hearing about the alchemists who tried to make gold from cheaper metals, concoct secret potions, and conjure incantations in dark little rooms. When I got home, I melted my brother's tin soldiers in an old pan on the kitchen stove.

I was fascinated with The Cloisters' ancient carved doors, marble altars, stained glass, and tapestries. But I was surprised when my aunt, whose manners equaled her intelligence, interrupted a woman sitting at an easel copying a fresco of the Madonna and her child. She asked the woman why she was copying a painting instead of painting an original one. The artist smiled. "Do you play the piano?" she asked. My aunt nodded. "Then you know the answer," the artist continued. "You play the work of famous composers just as I paint the work of famous artists." My aunt said, "I understand," but she was looking at me to make sure that I understood or would at least remember so that I would understand one day.

I wasn't sure what the point was. I hated my piano lessons. My weekly art class was a trial redeemed only by the messes I could make with finger paints, scissors, yarn, and glue.

> *The Lord will ... comfort all her waste places, and will make her wilderness like Eden, her desert like the garden of the Lord; joy and gladness will be found in her, thanksgiving and the voice of song.*
>
> ISAIAH 51:3

Still, I would get "itchy," my aunt's word for "bored." Aunt Esther lead me through a huge, bronze door and into a garden she called a "cloister."

"In these places the nuns had their garden in medieval times," she said. The flowers smelled nice, but I liked the woods, where I could pretend to be a princess, much better than I liked gardens.

"And this is the herb garden," she said leading me to a patch of greenery behind a marble fountain. The smell was stronger here, but the plants didn't even have flowers. I knew she was going to say it, that I was getting itchy again, so I was surprised when she sat me on a little stone bench and began to talk about herbs and their uses by cooks and physicians. Each herb has a legend, a story, she said. I was no longer itchy. I wanted to hear more, but the closing bell chimed. I plucked a rosemary leaf and tucked it into my pocket. Rosemary, I now knew, was for remembrance. In the museum's gift shop, my aunt bought me a little book on the history and lore of herbs.

When our week's visit was over, my father picked me up. My aunt carefully wrapped the little clay pots we had planted with herb seeds and set them in a cardboard box in the backseat. From the thyme to the cilantro, I knew what my herbs could be used for and how they were used

In the Middle Ages, women made necklaces of rosemary to preserve their youth and to attract elves. It was believed that a fresh rosemary twig tucked under your pillow would drive away nightmares and would come in handy when those little elves start tugging at your sheets. Rosemary was widely grown in the kitchen gardens of medieval housewives, perhaps because of the old folk saying: "Where rosemary flourishes, the woman rules."

in the Middle Ages. I even knew how to spell them. My brother's tin soldiers were safe now. I used the old pan to brew tea, which I flavored with lemon verbena and mint leaves—and as much sugar as I could get away with.

Since then, I have always had an herb garden, from clay pots on windowsills in dorm rooms and apartments to the cloister-size herb garden in my backyard today. The alchemist in me will tell you that if you let cilantro go to seed, you will harvest coriander; the poet in me will tell you that every whiff of rosemary reminds me of the precious aunt God blessed me with.

Women's Pews

On our vacation to Belize, my 20-year-old daughter Pam and I boarded a boat for the trip from our island resort to the mainland to see some Mayan ruins. I missed the scramble for seat cushions to watch molten sun flow across the sea. Pam sat on a seat cushion and pointed to the splintery wood seat beside her.

I sat on my folded gray sweatshirt across from Robert and Macy, an elderly couple we

> *And this, our life, exempt from public haunt, finds tongues in trees, books in the running brooks, sermons in stones, and good in everything.*
>
> WILLIAM SHAKESPEARE

had dinner with the night before. "If this vessel sinks, you're sharing your personal flotation device with your poor old mom," I said, winking at Pam.

Macy smiled at my joke and slipped her arm through her husband's. "You can have Robert's. He's an excellent swimmer. Olympic team— almost."

Robert stroked her thigh and smiled. "Macy, that was 40 years ago." Her tan skin hung loosely on the hand he seemed reluctant to remove. Her wrinkles, gray hair, mottled skin, and bifocals did not hide her relaxed and peaceful beauty. I saw Macy as Robert did, the young girl who loved him and the old woman who still did.

While sweat trickled down my back, saltwater splattered my arms and face as the boat sped along. The sea roughened. My teeth clacked together as we headed toward the mainland's jungle. Macy linked her arm through Robert's. I wondered what memories they had strung together like pearls on a strong thread. Robert stroked Macy's check and held her wind-whipped hair from her forehead. Today was one of their pearls.

The boat shot into the inlet; the motor whined and then stopped. The guide pointed over the edge of the boat. Stingrays carpeted the river bottom, moving with the current, their barbed tails sheaved in shadows.

At the Mayan ruins, 20-year-old Pam was halfway up the Sun God's temple before I noticed that she and the tour group had left me standing on the grass that covered a stone court-yard. The Sun God temple was the tallest struc-ture among the ruins. *That figures*, I thought, striding toward the Moon Goddess temple.

On the shady side, the stone steps were mossy and damp. I wanted to take off my shoes; climb on bare, calloused feet; and dance on the grass. After I pulled myself up a steep step halfway up the tem-ple, I stood on a platform. I looked over my shoul-der. Pam was on top of the sun temple, aiming her camera at me. I was struck with the feeling that Pam was looking at me from a distance of cen-

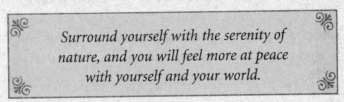

> *Surround yourself with the serenity of nature, and you will feel more at peace with yourself and your world.*

turies, looking at an ancestral grandmother whose feet were planted in the black, fertile dirt. With renewed vigor, I resumed my climb.

I stood above the tree line at the waist-high temple wall. The wind was sweeping leaves from the altar and the stones around the perimeter. I touched one of those stones. It was warm from the sun, but, I knew, beneath the scientific truth vibrated a more ancient one. These stones were women's pews. I sat on a stone and prayed, "Jesus, bless my daughter, Pam. Give her a man who loves like Robert. Let her age like Macy. Make her memories pearls."

It was a start. It had been two months since Pam's fiancé had broken their engagement and my daughter's heart. Macy and Robert were God's way of reminding me that love—lasting love—truly exists.

◆━◀○▶━◆

Father, thank you for the fine, gold nets hanging from my backyard bushes. I know they are spiderwebs. My little girl thought it would be fun to throw a handful of sparkles in the air. When she saw the way they landed on the spider's strong, delicate lace I know you saw the look on her face. And you are smiling with me. Thank you for sending this precious moment and sharing it with us.

◆━◀○▶━◆

A Perfect Summer Day

Visiting my Uncle Terry never felt like a duty, and it was usually a pleasure to drive 30 miles to see him. On a particular Saturday in June, I woke up thinking about him, and I was soon in my car on the way to the nursing home. In my purse were a photo of his mother, taken when he was young, a bag of gumdrops, and a book of Wordsworth's poems.

He had not seen this photo of his mother in more than a year, and he could not recognize her face, but I wanted him to know that he was somebody's beloved son. While he ate the gumdrops, he could not remember the person who brought him a sweet sticky treat now and then. The poems were a new idea. He had been a poet of some repute, and I thought the rhythm of poetry might vibrate beneath the thick cobwebs veiling his memory.

He was eating breakfast when I arrived and made no sign of recognition when I sat at the table with him. I smiled when I saw the computer printout of his breakfast order. "Extra portions" was underlined and circled. He had never been a big eater or even an enthusiastic

> The Lord will guide you continually, and satisfy
> your needs in parched places, and make your bones
> strong; and you shall be like a watered garden, like
> a spring of water, whose waters never fail.
>
> ISAIAH 58:11

one. Food was just a refueling stop on his way
to his next poem. But when he lost his poetry,
eating became a pleasure. As far as I could tell, it
was his only one.

After breakfast and his dessert of gumdrops,
we walked through the lovely grounds of the
nursing home. He held my hand, not in affec-
tion or for any other reason except my hand was
simply there. Wordsworth's poems stayed tucked
under my arm. I knew some lines by heart. "I
wandered lonely as a cloud," I said pointing to
the sky. He showed no sign of recognition of
poem or cloud.

We continued along the path. I recited, "All
things that love the sun are out of doors; the sky
rejoices in the morning's birth." He plodded
along, not looking at the sun, which I noticed
was now covered by the cloud. A few raindrops
fell. I led him into a little gazebo and sat across
from him on a wooden bench. Rain fell lightly
around the gazebo. I wanted to cry. But some-

thing stirred him. He cocked his head like a bird and walked to the edge of the gazebo. Rain fell on his face, and he smiled.

I thanked God that my uncle had enjoyed three pleasures today: a hearty breakfast, gum-drops, and the feel of rain on his face. He sat back down. While we waited for the shower to stop, I opened the book of poems. The first lines I turned to were these: "There is a comfort in the strength of love; 'Twill make a thing endurable, which else would overset the brain, or break the heart." I read the poem to my uncle who still looked like the poet in the author photo of his last book. On the ride home, I realized that the words of a long dead poet were God's words for me, not my uncle, on that perfect summer day.

⋅◆⋅►◀◯►◀⋅◆⋅

Dear Lord, thank you for giving all of us an equal measure of your blessings: shining sun, singing birds, and the full moon resting extravagantly on a black velvet sky. Gold coins are small change, no matter how brightly they shine, compared to nature's grandeur that your children never hoard, but simply share. Thank you for the wonder of your creation and for how it often heals our weary spirits. Amen

⋅◆⋅►◀◯►◀⋅◆⋅

Chapter Six

Silver Linings and Pots of Gold

Life's most treasured blessings often arise from the ashes of adversity and the depths of despair.

*I*t has been said that upon each and every life, a little rain must fall. Some lives experience far more rain than others, but for those who have the wisdom to look for the rainbow after the rain and for the pot of gold at the end of the rainbow, blessings from God abound.

> *I will no longer run from sorrow, for I've discovered pain can inspire.*
> *Many love songs, powerful poems, marvelous masterpieces were forged in times of adversity.*

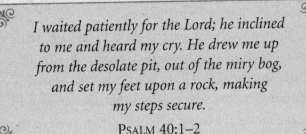
Life's most important lessons are often learned only as a result of overcoming great obstacles and accepting the challenges—both big and small—that we encounter with courage, determination, and faith. God never gives us more than we can handle, and he always gives us exactly what we need to contribute to our growth, our wisdom, our humanity, and our understanding. Even the pain of tragedy and loss holds the power to transform us, to teach us, and to make us into better people, but only if we see God's blessing during the current crisis.

Without darkness, we would not recognize light. Without struggle, there would be little to appreciate when good times arrive. Without conflict, we would never rise to become stronger, more tolerant, and compassionate people. Miracles, true miracles, occur when we move beyond the pain and fear to the profound and lasting changes that suffering brings.

Strive to always see the good in the bad, sense the harmony in any conflict, find the lesson in the "stressin'," and keep your eyes and hearts focused on the silver linings that appear around each cloud. Then we will realize that even in the darkest moments of our lives, we are deeply loved and abundantly blessed by God.

⋄—⟨O⟩—⋄

Dear God, help me see the silver lining that surrounds this dark cloud hanging over my head today. I know that this, too, shall pass, but right now my courage is weak. Let me feel your presence, even in this situation. Thank you, God, for I know that you are always near.

⋄—⟨O⟩—⋄

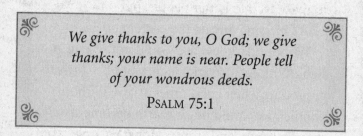

We give thanks to you, O God; we give thanks; your name is near. People tell of your wondrous deeds.

PSALM 75:1

What Really Matters

I lost everything in that fire—everything, that is, except for a small photo album I had managed to grab in my haste to get out before the flames tore into our cul-de-sac and ravaged what was once my little "neck of the woods."

The actual loss didn't even hit me until two days later while I was staying at my parents' home. I turned on the news and saw my street—or what was once my street—leveled into a field of smoking ash. The newscaster was standing in front of my house, and the only thing remaining was a big chunk of the front door. I broke down and cried like a baby, realizing that every material object I owned was gone forever.

My mom came and sat with me on the couch, and she told me she would go with me the next

⋆ ◆ ⊶〈○〉⊷ ◆ ⋆

God, I give you thanks and praise for the richness of my life and for the lessons I have learned from my struggles. Without those lessons, I would not be the person I am today nor have the blessings I have. So thank you, God, for the good and the bad, for better and for worse.

⋆ ◆ ⊶〈○〉⊷ ◆ ⋆

> *Hope and patience are two sovereign remedies for all, the surest reposals, the softest cushions to lean on in adversity.*
>
> ROBERT BURTON

day to walk through the debris. I couldn't even respond because it hurt so much. I hated to think of myself as so materialistic, but when you lose everything, you have to let yourself grieve. The pain was deep, and I was just not strong enough to "buck it up" and smile my way through it.

The next morning, my mom and dad both drove me to my home site, and, hand in hand, the three of us walked through the debris pile. Each time we found a little trinket or item that had not been burned beyond recognition, we all literally thanked God aloud and giggled like schoolchildren with the sheer joy of each memory that rose from the ashes. By the time we had walked the entire lot, we had accumulated three boxes of stuff: things like forks, knickknacks, and even a few picture frames with photos intact.

The funny thing was, each item we found had such a profound personal meaning for me, unlike things like clothing or books or even my computer. It was as if the fire was trying to tell me something; that my life was too cluttered, and now here I was, left with what really matters, what really lasts.

I went home with my parents that night, and we stayed up until 2:00 A.M. recounting memories of my childhood and talking about our lives in ways we never had before. I prayed that night, giving thanks to God for everything I had, and, surprisingly enough, for everything I had lost. I even thanked God for the fire itself and the powerful sense of clarity it had given me. I felt such overwhelming hope and gratitude and a certainty that my future was going to be bright and filled with blessings to come.

•᚛＋᚛（O）᚜＋᚜•

FROM THE ASHES
We look for silver linings
Wrapped around the darkest cloud,
And seek the pretty rainbows
On those gray days of our life.
For in our faith we've come to know
That daylight follows night,
And blessings always rise up from
Our struggles and our strife.

•᚛＋᚛（O）᚜＋᚜•

Failing to Succeed

Bob never imagined that the business he had put 20 years of his life into would end like this. He had lost more than one million dollars worth of business to a competitor, and with hard times already making it more difficult to keep afloat, he knew what he had to do.

He began to lay off the remaining few employees who had managed to stick around, even amid word of a sinking ship. He gave them what little severance he could and thanked them for everything they had done. Even though he was watching his livelihood slip away, he realized with deep gratitude that these people had helped him in countless ways. He thanked God for the blessing of their years of service, but he still felt a certain bitterness that he had to watch them go.

On the night when the doors were closed for good, Bob went home and wept silently in the bathroom. His loving wife, Christy, knew that he was suffering, but she gave him the space he needed. She worried that this terrible turn of events would damage Bob's already delicate heart. He had suffered a heart attack a year before from stress over his struggling business,

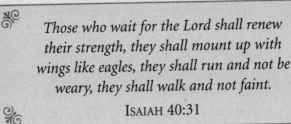

Those who wait for the Lord shall renew their strength, they shall mount up with wings like eagles, they shall run and not be weary, they shall walk and not faint.

ISAIAH 40:31

and Christy hoped that the failure of his business wouldn't be the final straw.

That night, Bob lay in bed praying silently. He thanked God for the business; for, indeed, he was grateful for the good years and for all he had learned. But he also asked God to bless him with some sense of new direction, for he felt more lost and alone than ever before in his life. What would he do? Where would the money come from? He didn't want Christy to go back to work outside the home, not when her pottery business was just taking off.

Eventually Bob fell asleep. In his dreams, he ran from something just at his heels, something he could not see. He was filled with fear until, in one final dream, he turned and faced the thing that was chasing him.

Bob awoke abruptly and sat up in bed. It was 4:00 A.M. Christy was fast asleep. Bob went into their home office and turned on the computer. He got onto the Internet and spent the rest of

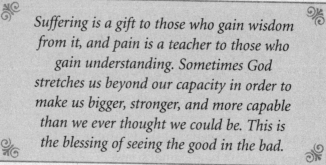

Suffering is a gift to those who gain wisdom from it, and pain is a teacher to those who gain understanding. Sometimes God stretches us beyond our capacity in order to make us bigger, stronger, and more capable than we ever thought we could be. This is the blessing of seeing the good in the bad.

the morning researching an idea that had come to him in the night, an idea that filled him with excitement.

Within a few months, Bob and Christy were running dual home-based businesses: Christy selling her pottery creations, and Bob doing something he had always wanted to do but never thought he could. He became an online consultant to new business ventures, using his expertise and knowledge to help others avoid the mistakes he had made. He had always dreamed of being his own boss, and now he thanked God for blessing him with another opportunity to live that dream again.

The failure of his business had been one of the best things that had ever happened to him, and he knew that his future would be successful with God and his wife behind him.

A Home of Her Own

For the fifth time that month, Jackie had been forced to lie to a creditor. Now she was facing possible foreclosure on the three-bedroom house she and her two children called home. Her husband had passed away from a stroke, and he had been self-employed, leaving Jackie with only a few thousand dollars in savings. Day care cost more than most jobs paid, and Jackie didn't have a trusted relative nearby she could leave the kids with.

She felt as though her foundation was being pulled out from under her. There was just no way she could come up with enough money each month to make their mortgage. The kids, ages two and three, were not yet in school, and Jackie had hoped they could grow up in the nice, new development where she and her husband had planned to live out the rest of their years.

The constant stress of having to dodge creditors was getting to her, and Jackie just couldn't

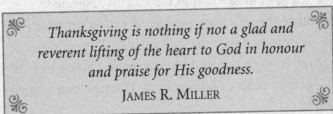

Thanksgiving is nothing if not a glad and reverent lifting of the heart to God in honour and praise for His goodness.

JAMES R. MILLER

HINDSIGHT IS 20/20

I asked God to take this yoke from me,
But he just plain refused.
I asked God to stop my suffering,
But he was not amused.
Seems God desired in his own way
To prosper me with good,
And strengthen me to do the things
I never thought I could.
If only I had trusted in him,
my wise and loving master,
I would have quickly seen the light
And learned the lessons faster.

take it anymore. She prayed to God to go ahead and do his will, and if his will was to take the house away, then so be it. She had faith in God and knew his plans for her weren't always what she would have chosen, but she still couldn't help feeling anxious over what the future held.

A realtor friend offered to help Jackie quickly sell her home to avoid foreclosure, especially since the area was considered a seller's market. Within two months, Jackie had sold her home for enough money to buy a smaller house in a nearby older neighborhood. The new mortgage would be much smaller, something Jackie could afford with her income from her husband's death benefit and the home-based business she was struggling to get off the ground. The neighborhood was definitely not the sparkly new one she had hoped to raise her kids in, but she realized that the stress of living above her means was destroying her happiness.

Jackie settled her children into their new home and saw how they loved the bigger backyard, something newer houses rarely offered. She felt encouraged by that simple blessing, which she had overlooked but her children had discovered immediately. They also pointed out a park, which was within walking distance. And during the next few days, several neighbors with children the same age as hers visited Jackie. They were all eager to befriend their newest resident.

Although she missed the bigger home she had loved and left, Jackie felt blessed not only that God had given her a new home that she could afford but also that he had provided plenty of amusements for her children. The biggest blessing was being able to go to bed at night free from the gut-wrenching stress of wondering how to make the next mortgage payment. By trusting in God, what looked like a terrible loss had turned into something positive...a home she could truly call her own.

Traffic Jam

Sara swore under her breath. The traffic reporter had just announced that a major accident was blocking the freeway and that commuters should expect a several-hour delay. Her day had been awful from the start. Now she couldn't even get home to relax without having to deal with even more stress.

Changing radio stations, Sara became more frustrated by the minute as she searched for a way to keep her mind occupied. She could see by the looks on the faces of motorists beside her that she was not the only one boiling with impatience. Everybody looked miffed. After about a half-hour of cursing her fate and wondering why she didn't listen to her first instinct and take the

> *We know that all things work together for good for those who love God, who are called according to his purpose.*
>
> ROMANS 8:28

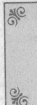

When life doesn't go according to our plan, and calamity strikes, our true character is revealed. How we handle adversity signals what kind of person we are deep inside.

side streets, she resigned herself to her situation and settled on a call-in radio talk show.

The host was a popular local woman who had made millions designing her own linens. Since Sara had a secret desire to be an interior designer, she listened attentively. When the host introduced her guest, Sara almost popped out of her seat and through her sunroof. The name was instantly recognizable, and Sara listened to confirm that the voice was really Jenny Cameron—her best friend from college.

Sara had always dreamed of getting in touch with Jenny. They had lost contact when Jenny moved to the East Coast to start her design business fresh out of college. A few e-mails had passed between them, but eventually each woman became caught up in the busyness of their own lives. It had been almost ten years since Sara had heard from Jenny.

Now here she was, coming to her live over the radio. The show host gave out the call-in number, and Sara grabbed her cell phone and dialed.

Within minutes, the host had her on the air, and Sara asked an innocuous question about the use of color. Jenny answered and then asked if she knew the caller since her voice was so familiar. Sara told Jenny her identity, and the two chatted live on the air like silly schoolgirls. Eventually, the host had to steer the conversation back to design but not before Jenny promised to call Sara. She asked Sara to stay on the line and give the studio assistant her phone number.

A few days later, Sara and Jenny were making plans to get together. Sara realized that had she not been stuck in traffic on that fateful day, she never would have heard the voice of her old friend and reconnected. She thanked God for the blessing of being in the right place at the right time, and promised never to complain about traffic jams again.

—◦—

God, I pray to you today that I may be blessed with a stronger faith. For with faith, all else will come to me in good time. For with faith, I will no longer feel frightened or alone during times of darkness and despair. Thank you, God, for the precious gift of my belief in you.

—◦—

A Welcome Flood

Brenda was ready to scream. This was the third time in as many months that the kitchen sink had flooded, and now water poured out from under the counter all over the floor. Panicking, she called her husband, Rob, who told her to call his friend, Joe, a plumber.

An hour later, Brenda watched as Joe crawled out from under the sink, his face looking grim. "Not good, Brenda, not good," he mumbled, then explained that he would have to replace the drain-pipe and redo the shoddy plumbing job that the previous homeowners had left.

The job would cost a pretty penny, and Brenda felt crushed. Their car had also broken

---

AFFIRMATIONS FOR INNER PEACE

I see the positive in every negative situation.
I discern the lesson in every challenging occurrence.
I feel the presence of God in every painful event.
I know the power of his love for me
in every difficult experience.
I hear his gentle guidance in every fearful endeavor.
God is my silver lining, my precious pot of gold.

down the week before to the tune of $400, and now they were going to have to pinch their already pinched budget even more. With only Rob working, times were pretty tough, but it had to be done.

"Hey, it could be worse," Joe joked. "You could have had a slab leak. Those are really brutal." Brenda just couldn't bring herself to share Joe's sense of optimism.

In a few days, Joe returned with all the necessary parts and began the work. As he pulled up the baseboard under the sink, he called out to Brenda, pointing out to her a large spot of darkened wood. He then spoke the one word that sent chills down Brenda's spine.

"Mold."

Brenda held her breath as he continued working. Her neighbor had just spent several thousand dollars having a mold problem rectified, and she knew that she and Rob could never afford to deal with the same situation.

Joe kept shaking his head, and Brenda felt her legs turning to jelly. "Please God," she prayed silently, "Don't let it be so bad, not right now, not when we are struggling so badly already."

Finally, Joe came up for air and looked at Brenda. He smiled.

"You're lucky. The mold hasn't spread. I can easily take care of it."

Brenda felt a whoosh of air escape her lungs as she thanked God for the piece of good news.

"Good thing for you this little flood happened when it did," Joe said, "or we might not have caught the mold until it was too late."

As Joe went out to his truck to get his tools, Brenda leaned against the counter and sighed with relief. She laughed out loud when she realized that God had blessed them with a flood and saved them from drowning!

* * *

Heavenly Father, I thank you for the challenges and obstacles you have placed before me. They were difficult, and they caused me great pain, but the end result is a stronger, more faithful, compassionate "me." Thank you for helping me find the rainbow after the cold, dark storm.

Amen

* * *

Chapter Seven

The Magic Moment

Living in the moment opens the heart to God's glorious gifts and bountiful blessings.

Where do you live? It is a powerful question when asked in terms of where your focus is. Do you live in the past, held back by regrets over what was and bitterness toward what might have been? Are you locked in the future, worrying about what might come to be? Where does your spirit call home?

To really feel alive and to truly experience the overwhelming evidence of God's blessings around us requires us to live in the moment. In the here and now, everything is always as it should be, and God's love is never more deeply felt than when we are focused on what is right in front of us. Whether we are doing the dishes, working in the garden, playing with our children, washing the car, or giving a speech to thousands of employees, we need to be totally focused on where we are, whom we are with, and what we are doing. Thus we open up to a greater awareness of our unity and connection with everything around us.

When we stress out over the past or the future, we close ourselves off to the wonder and magic of the *now*, for God's presence is palpable and his handiwork is visible in the tiniest details. Suddenly, we sense with our spirit what our eyes have never seen before—a world that is vibrant and alive with light, love, and the pure possibility that exists only in the moment at hand. We achieve

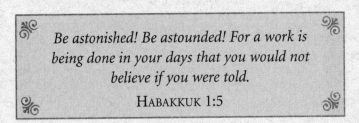

Be astonished! Be astounded! For a work is being done in your days that you would not believe if you were told.

HABAKKUK 1:5

clarity of vision that is not possible when we are locked in the fears and doubts of being somewhere other than where we are right now.

Living in the moment banishes all despair about the past and all anxiety about the future. Living in the moment gives us the profound ability to accept anything that comes our way with humility, courage, and a deep sense of gratitude that is centered in the joy of just being alive. What an amazing gift the moment is, filled with the blessings of a universe flowing with God's love and grace.

That is why it is called "the present."

God, I am amazingly blessed today with all good things you have placed into my life, so my prayer is not for me but for those who are not able to see the good that is in their midst. May they have eyes like mine, open to the miracles you perform all around us. Thank you for each one of these blessings.

Amen

Sammy the Stressbuster

Being a mother of three was sometimes more than Gail could handle. With two older children in school, she found herself dealing with a toddler and the tornado of activity that surrounded him.

Little Sammy had just turned three, and he had the energy of triplets, often leaving Gail too tired to even put together a sentence. She was also trying to run a home-based accounting business, keep track of her older kids' activities, and make what little time she could for her husband, John, her elderly mother who lived nearby, and for herself. Needless to say, it was Gail who often got the short shift. She was lucky if she had time to take a shower every other day.

The afternoons were the worst when Gail's energy reached an all-time low point, and today was no exception. Sammy hated to nap, and Gail

> *Each moment is sacred, for an entire life can be transformed in just one moment. Knowing that, we must expect miracles now, not in the future, for the now is all we truly have.*

put on a pot of coffee, knowing she would need it to get through to dinnertime. The phone kept ringing with some minor issue after another, and Gail felt at wits end when a neighbor dropped by unexpectedly to gossip about the rest of the neighborhood.

After her neighbor finally left, Gail realized that it was almost 3:00 P.M. and that she desperately needed to rest. Sammy, however, was still going full steam ahead. Gail picked him up firmly and carried him into his room. She told him to play quietly so she could lie on the bed for a few minutes. He protested for awhile, but Gail shook her head and walked away.

In her bedroom, Gail closed the blinds and laid down, hoping to catch even just ten minutes of sleep or something close to it, but her mind buzzed with thoughts, and her body refused to stop driving on eight cylinders. She tossed and turned, and she felt like crying.

Sammy came into her room and crawled up on the bed next to her. He snuggled into her body and gave her a soft kiss on the cheek.

"Can I rest with you, Mommy?" he asked, his big green eyes looking into hers. Gail felt herself melt with love for her little force of nature that God had given her, and she held him close. As she did, the stresses of the day simply melted away as well, and Gail and Sammy fell asleep together.

Gail awoke first, over an hour and a half later. She gazed down at little Sammy, still fast asleep, and stroked his hair. An overwhelming sense of inner peace filled her heart. She remained on the bed for awhile, feeling intense gratitude and love for her little trouper. She was tired, no doubt about it, but she knew right then that God had blessed her with this little boy and that if she just stayed focused on the present moment, she could handle anything— especially when she knew there was a piping hot pot of coffee waiting!

BLESSED ARE THOSE
Blessed are those who see blessings
In each and every day,
For sometimes it's the simple things
That help us on our way.
And sometimes it's the miracle
Of unexpected things,
That make our hearts leap skyward
And give our spirits wings.

Clear as a Bell

Whenever Roger was on the warpath, raging and screaming at everyone in the office, Bill automatically went on autopilot just to get through the workday. Sometimes Bill spent most of his days working at home just to avoid his boss, but he couldn't always avoid the office.

One day Bill heard Roger's screaming getting closer and knew he would be next in the line of fire. While he wondered why he ever took this job, he got up to quietly close and lock his office door, but before he could, Roger stormed in.

Bill tuned out. It was all he could do—all anybody at the company could do—just tune

 Blessings occur in the moments of our lives when we become acutely aware of our connection to God, to nature, and to others. In these moments, we awaken to the reality of our harmony with everything around us. In these moments, we see the splendor of creation dancing in the tiniest and simplest of things, and the wonder of God's love for us in the smallest and most inconsequential of events.

Roger out until his rage blew over, and then everything would be back to normal. Ten minutes later, Roger had moved on. Bill felt numb, frozen to his chair. Why, he kept asking himself, do I work here? What am I doing with my life?

The problem was, he spent too much time focused on the future, thinking about how much money he would need in order to retire comfortably. And so he rarely examined what he was feeling right now in this moment.

As he drove home from another harrowing day, he found himself stuck in a traffic jam, and he tuned out by listening to radio music. Not paying attention, he jumped when the driver behind him honked. Bill realized that the traffic had cleared in front of him and that he had been holding up a line of cars and angry drivers. For how long? He couldn't even say, for his mind has truly been somewhere else. In the flash of a second, Bill had a feeling of total clarity—a sense of being so in the moment that everything, including the cars whizzing by, seemed perfectly in focus and acutely present.

When he pulled into his driveway, Bill shut the engine and sat in his car for a few minutes. He felt entirely grounded, centered, and alert. He had been holding up traffic by being "somewhere else," and now the lesson truly hit home. He had been holding up HIS LIFE by being "somewhere else."

Bill got out of the car, thanking God for the blessing of clarity. He went into the house with a purpose, and the next day he quit his job to become a private consultant. The clarity stayed with him as long as he kept himself focused in the moment and on the powerful blessing of pure potential that each moment held.

◦•⊷◖O◗⊶•◦

Dear Lord, you have showered me with blessings. Yet often I have so much trouble seeing them. Help me stay focused on the joys of the present and the wonders of each moment. That is where you are, Lord, and I want to be where you are.

◦•⊷◖O◗⊶•◦

Dirty Dishes

I hated washing dishes more than anything, including dusting (and I had asthma). Standing still for an hour scraping food off of forks was not my idea of fun, but the small apartment I rented did not have a dishwasher. The only saving grace was a small window above the sink that looked out onto a park area, where children from the complex played and laughed and many of my neighbors often congregated on warm summer days.

As I grumbled over the dishes that had piled up, wishing I could be watching TV or reading a good book, I heard a loud cry and looked out the window just in time to see an elderly woman holding her head with one hand and pointing to the sky with the other. A crowd gathered to assist her, and I overheard her scream about how a big bird had swooped down from the sky and stolen her hat. The little old lady was fuming, and I distinctly heard her say some unkind words to the bird.

I stopped washing, caught up in the hilarious comedy going on outside, and suddenly I felt

In the magic of the present, we find evidence of God's existence in the details of our lives that we often otherwise ignore: the feel of the sun's warmth on our skin, the lovely song of a bird building a nest, the smell of fresh-baked bread from a neighbor's kitchen. These gentle reminders keep us focused on being fully alive and fully engaged in life. Yesterday is gone. Tomorrow may never come. Today is where we live.

> *You shall eat in plenty and be satisfied, and*
> *praise the name of the Lord your God, who*
> *has dealt wondrously with you.*
>
> JOEL 2:26

such a profound sense of being in the moment.
My hands dangled in the soapy water as I
watched children playing on a slide, two lovers
holding hands as they walked, and a little dog
jumping up to catch a thrown twig.

I was usually too busy fretting about the
future or regretting something stupid I did in
the past that I rarely felt as though I were truly
in control of my own life. But this feeling was
awesome, and I thanked God for everything I
was seeing, feeling, hearing, and smelling. The
intensity of the sensations was profound. Was
life always this way? Was I just missing it because
I was never in the present?

I knew that the feeling probably wouldn't last
and that the stresses and strains of the world
would once again take my poor mind hostage.
But for right now, I felt truly awake and alive
and blessed and grateful and loved and whole
and complete, standing there at the window,
doing nothing more than washing a bunch of
dirty dishes. "Thank you, Lord."

Holy Spirit, help me stop stressing out so much and to enjoy the simple pleasures of my life. Help me stay centered in the present and grounded in the moment at hand. Help me see the magic in everything I do today, even the drudgery.

One Step at a Time

After six months of intensive training, Dana was actually here at the starting line of the Sun City Marathon. She felt apprehensive, but her sister Lisa had run several marathons and was right beside her, ready to support her all the way to the finish line. This race was important to Dana. She had just lost her job, and her fiancé had left her for another woman he knew from his office. She needed the challenge and the self-confidence it would bring.

The starting gun went off, and the race began. Dana remembered all the advice she had received about getting off to a slow and steady pace, and by the first quarter mark, she was feeling in the groove, or the zone as Lisa called it.

By the halfway mark, however, Dana started to feel a terrible pain in her groin. She had suffered an injury more than a decade ago, and she hoped this wasn't related. She motioned for Lisa to go on ahead, and Lisa took off to try to beat her former race time. Alone, Dana tried not to think about the pain, which was now a persistent throb. She desperately wanted to finish this race and prove to herself that she could do it.

Feeling that she was letting herself down, Dana slowed her pace and even began to walk. She wanted to keep running, but she had to admit the walking made her groin pain lessen. Several runners had also either dropped out by this point or slowed to a walk. Dana caught the eye of an attractive man walking past her, and he smiled and winked. "One step at a time!" he yelled.

Dana continued walking, and as she did, she sensed God helping her mind to become sharp and focused on each step. The physical exertion was enough to deal with, and she simply could not think too much or she might give up. Her groin was beginning to throb again, and she felt dizzy and out of sorts. She forced herself to focus on the road beneath her feet and the sound of her breathing, and she silently prayed to God to help her reach the finish line, whether she had to walk, crawl, or hop on one foot.

> *Know the true value of time; snatch, seize,*
> *and enjoy every moment of it.*
> LORD CHESTERTON

About 500 yards from the finish line, Dana felt overcome by her pain, and she stumbled. Closing her eyes and gritting her teeth, she forced herself up and kept moving, even as her body quivered from weakness. She could see the finish line up ahead, and Lisa waving at her.

"One step at a time," Dana said out loud and kept her awareness on her feet, one and then the other and then the other. The rest of the world faded away, and Dana felt only her two feet touch the firmness of the road. Dana felt blessed with a burst of new energy and actually ran, pain and all, through the final 50 yards, finishing the race with a whoop of joy before she fell to the ground.

Lisa was at her side, offering help while congratulating her. But it was a man's arms that held Dana as she regained her equilibrium, and she looked up into the smiling face of the guy she had seen on the road.

"One step at a time," Dana whispered.

"Always works for me," the man said with a grin, helping Dana to her feet.

Dana celebrated that night with her new friend, Josh, over dinner. She had done it, by taking one step at a time... with a little help from above.

❖—◁◦▷—❖

TOO MANY TO COUNT

I sit and count my blessings
As the evening stars appear,
One blessing for each star I see,
The distant and the near.
Soon my heart feels lighter
When I come to realize
That I have way more blessings than
There are stars up in the sky.

❖—◁◦▷—❖

Pulling Weeds

Mary loved her garden more than any other part of her beautiful home. She had spent two years getting everything just the way she wanted it, and she considered it her sanctuary. But as much as she loved planting her flowers and watching them bloom, she despised weeding. Because she couldn't afford to hire a gardener, each weekend she had to get on her hands and knees to do the dirty deed, constantly grumbling about how much time she was wasting and what she could and should be doing instead.

The dandelions drove her crazy; there were so many of them. The work was tedious, and she felt rushed to get it done before the hot noonday sun made outdoor activity impossible. Resigning herself to the task at hand, Mary grabbed each weed by its base, pulled, and tossed it into a yard waste receptacle positioned behind her.

Grab, pull, toss. Grab, pull, toss. Soon, Mary was feeling the rhythm of her work, and she began to feel better. The morning sun was warm but was not yet a problem, and she often stopped to watch a butterfly float above her flower beds.

Grab, pull, toss. Grab, pull, toss. Mary stopped suddenly, weed in hand, a silly thought playing through her mind. Wouldn't it be great, she imagined, if I could make a game out of this to make the time go by faster?

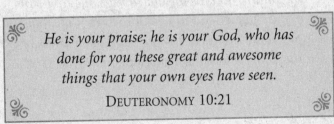

He is your praise; he is your God, who has done for you these great and awesome things that your own eyes have seen.

DEUTERONOMY 10:21

Mary reached for the next weed, and as she pulled it out, she counted a blessing. "Thank you, God, for my garden." Then, with the next weed, she continued, "Thank you, God, for my strong hands." Then, "Thank you, God, for the gift of water." "Thank you, God, for the warm sun that grows my flowers." She ended with, "Thank you, God, for these weeds and for the reminders of all the good things in my life."

By the time Mary had finished the job, she had pulled more than a hundred weeds and counted out more than a hundred things she was deeply grateful for. Her heart was joyful, and her spirit was light as air as she gathered up her tools and headed inside to clean up. Never again would she grumble about weeding, not when she could spend the time in her favorite place, her garden, counting her bountiful blessings and basking in the warmth of the morning sun.

God, thank you for the little things, the moments of pure joy when I am so absorbed in life that I forget the regrets of the past and the worries of the future. I love these precious moments, God. They make my spirit soar.
Amen

Chapter Eight

All That I Am and Hope to Be

We can thank God for what we are, for our potential, and for our purpose in life.

*E*very day I thank God that I'm alive and that I can open the shades each morning to see what the day will be like. I love to stretch and check to see if all my joints and muscles still work. I do my daily chores with a thankful heart just to be here (well, most days anyway).

As a child I had asthma and could hardly breathe. Some nights I thought I'd die. And so breathing is a blessing for me—just to feel air move smoothly in and out of my lungs. I'm glad to be here. I'm glad my friends and family are here. I'm glad there's a universe full of unique and amazing individuals out there because every person is a blessing, and I'm thankful God made us all.

> One day a little boy said, "I want to fly. I want to be a pilot." His friends teased him. His teacher told him to be more practical. His parents said to be realistic. The little boy didn't get discouraged though. He didn't give up. He kept trying, and today he's flying.

Everyone has gifts—things we do well. Everyone has dreams and hopes to keep us trying. And everyone has troubles and flaws that remind us that we aren't perfect. We're only human—and what a wonderful thing that is to be.

Above all else, I think, we are made to love and be loved. A friend once said, "Not loving is like not breathing." I can understand that. Breathing is life, and so is loving. We are here to love one another and to love God—and to thank him just for putting us here!

* ❖ ◁◇▷ ❖ *

Dear Lord, please help us be what you want us to be. Help us believe in ourselves and trust in you to help get us where we need to go. Help us be the very best that we can be each and every day of our lives.

* ❖ ◁◇▷ ❖ *

Mud Pies and Presidents

Watching the children play, Lori wondered what she should do with her life.

Mom had said it best: "You can't spend your whole life being a glorified babysitter, Lori Anne. You've got to get out there and do something big, something important, something that matters in the world."

Yes, Mom was probably right, but Lori didn't have a clue what to do differently. She hated the thought of going back to school for another degree. School had not agreed with her, and she sure hadn't enjoyed a single moment of classes, research papers, and exams. Every weekend, she searched the want ads, looking for a different job, something, as Mom put it, "with a future."

"Don't get discouraged, Lori Anne," Mom told her every week. "Something good will come along. You just need to keep hunting for it. Be ready when it shows up. For instance, look at this ad for a legal secretary. You could do that."

Mom was always hopeful over the ads she found each week, but Lori just couldn't get interested. The really discouraging part was that she loved her job. She hadn't told Mom that, but

Lori loved being around the little children. She enjoyed playing with them, singing with them, teaching them rhymes, and laughing with them.

Walking into the room each morning, her spirits lifted at the sight of the children. She loved the way their eyes lit up when they saw her. She loved seeing the world through their eyes and seeing tiny, magical moments that adults usually missed—the world at knee level. She'd helped the little ones discover nature, gluing leaves to sheets of poster board, and catching sight of a robin on its nest. Every day brought something new and something joyous.

Being with the children made Lori feel more alive than anything else she'd ever done. She'd had dozens of part-time jobs over the years—waitressing, cashiering, nurse's aid. You name it, she'd tried it. But nothing brought the pleasure this job did. The pay wasn't great, though, and as Mom constantly told her, it was really just "glorified babysitting, something a teenager would do."

Then one day, her boss noticed Lori's anxiety and asked what was wrong.

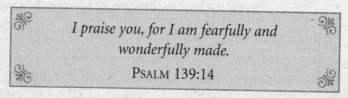

I praise you, for I am fearfully and wonderfully made.

Psalm 139:14

"My mom says I need to find a better job, something more important, something that really matters."

Her boss smiled then. "Look around you, Lori. What do you see?"

Lori saw the children fitting blocks together, learning to share, laughing, singing, and growing. "I see kids playing," Lori said.

"No," her boss told her. "What you see is the future. You see doctors and lawyers, stockbrokers, accountants, research biologists. You might even see a president out there. Lori, there is no more important job in the world than the one you have right now. You are helping these little ones reach for their future. You are giving them a chance to begin reaching for their dreams. Without day-care workers and preschool teachers, who would help shape their lives?"

Lori felt a shiver of awe shoot through her. All these little ones, God had placed them in her hands. They learned from her. She cheered them on when they tried for a goal, and she urged them not to give up when it got tough. She helped them be their best. She gave them encouragement and love every day along with their milk and crackers.

"Think about it," her boss said. "How much more important can a job be than using the gift

God has given you by helping the future President of the United States learn to tie his or her shoelaces and play fair?"

As her boss walked away, Lori grinned. It was true; one of those children making mud pies in the play yard might someday be deciding the future of the world!

ONLY ONE
I am a miracle—
there's only one of me.
There aren't any extras,
not two or three.
I am one of a kind—
God has broken the mold.
I eagerly watch for
my life to unfold.
I dream of flying;
I reach for the sky.
Why not, after all?
I might as well try!

Tawni and Jake

Pushing open the hospital door, Tawni stuck her head inside and grinned at the kid in the bed.

In this life, anything is possible. Who knows what we can become if we never give up, never let go, and never stop trying and reaching and believing in ourselves and in our God. Our potential is endless—a wonder, a delight, and a hope forever.

"Hi," she called. "You want a visitor today?"

The kid, Jason, popped upright in his bed, showing more energy than he had all day. "Yeah, sure, come on in." But he wasn't looking at Tawni. He looked past her at about knee level, watching for her companion, Jake, the wonder dog.

When Tawni first appeared at Jason's door, she had introduced her dog. "This is Jake, the wonder dog. I call him a wonder dog because it's a wonder he can walk and breathe at the same time. He's not the brightest bulb in the lamp, but he's a love."

Tawni and Jake sat around visiting for a good long time, and Jason got to hug Jake while enjoying Jake's wet tongue on his face. When it was time for Tawni and Jake to go, he hated to see them leave and called out, "Come back soon, okay?"

"Sure thing," Tawni promised. "Count on us. We'll be back."

Then Tawni and Jake headed down the hall for the next stop on her list. From room to room she went, taking Jake along, lifting hearts wherever they stopped to visit awhile. All the nurses knew them. If the rules said no dogs, not one of the nurses recalled that rule. Nobody argued about having a dog there. No matter how much fur Jake shed or even if he had an occasional accident on the hall floor, nobody fussed.

One new young nurse on duty that day asked about the pair. "What's with the dog anyway?"

The regular nurses filled her in. "Jake's special. He loves our patients. He slobbers on them, sheds fur everywhere, trips over his own two feet, and generally makes a fool of himself. But the kids are crazy about him. He cheers them up, and sometimes that means a lot. They get better faster when Jake's around. He's our secret weapon."

"What about Tawni? What's the deal there?" asked the new nurse. "Why does she do this?"

The other nurses got quiet, their faces serious and sad. "Tawni's the greatest blessing this ward ever had," one of the other nurses told her. "She understands these kids. She cares about them. She brings them treats, knows all their names, and prays for them. When things get bad, she comes and holds their parents' hands."

The new young nurse nodded. But the story wasn't done yet. She could tell by the way nobody looked straight at her, the way the other nurses became quieter still.

One of them explained the whole story: "Tawni's okay now. She's hanging in there, but she used to be on this ward herself. Nobody knew if she'd live or die; it was that bad. Even then, she reached out to everybody else. She tried to take care of us, you know, while she was fighting for her own life. She's one special person."

"And you know what?" the older nurse told the young one, "That klutzy Jake's a survivor, too. Tawni got him from the animal shelter. He was sick even then. He's had cancer, too, just like the kids on the ward. Maybe that's why he's so special to them. They're quite a pair those two. God couldn't have sent better angels."

The young nurse said a prayer of gratitude while quietly sweeping up a drift of fur Jake had left behind. It was such a small price to pay for such a great blessing.

* ◆ ◄O►◆ *

Oh, Lord, I see a world full of people. Everyone is unique. Yet we are all part of one another, too. All connected. All part of one family. All yours!

* ◆ ◄O►◆ *

Best at Loving

Years ago my husband drove a school bus. He saw the job as much more than driving. It was a way of reaching out to others. He drove a bus for physically challenged children. There was a lift for wheelchairs, and he always had an aide on the bus to help in case of emergency. The kids ranged in age and ability, but all had experienced some form of disability.

Some had experienced birth defects or injuries. Some suffered from serious illnesses. Their abilities varied. Some were more seriously disabled than others. My husband became attached to them all. He knew their ages, interests, and capabilities. He called them all by name and joked with them. One child nicknamed my husband "Hat" because of the large cowboy hat he wore.

Several of these special kids had been diagnosed with such severe problems that doctors advised they be shut away in institutions.

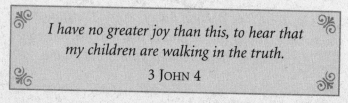

I have no greater joy than this, to hear that my children are walking in the truth.

3 JOHN 4

One doctor even described one little boy as nothing but a vegetable, who would never speak, never move normally, and never do anything for himself.

What I liked best about those kids is that they defied the doctors. They defied the rules that said they would never be able to do so many things. The boy whose doctor said he'd be a vegetable all his life rode on my husband's bus. He took some extra time to get aboard the bus, but he did it. He smiled, laughed, had a vocabulary of dozens of words, and seemed to thoroughly enjoy his school time.

Most assuredly he was not a vegetable. He was a wonderful, energetic, happy child. Perhaps he would never reach goals that many other children tried for, but he was far exceeding the expectations of his doctors. He was eagerly stretching to his limits and beyond.

My husband told me about "his kids" every day. He celebrated their achievements with them and encouraged them to do their very best. He loved those kids, and they loved him right back.

Through my husband's eyes I got to know these special children God had created. I loved to hear how they went beyond what anyone expected of them and the way they kept at tasks

> *We come in all shapes and sizes. All colors and kinds. We are big and small, fast and slow, rich and poor. And everything in between. There is no defining us, no setting limits to what we can do, and what we can be. We are different from one another in endless ways, yet alike in all that matters. We are not perfect and never will be, but we accept each other anyway. We are here for one another. We are humanity, and we are blessed.*

that took all their concentration and how they succeeded at their assigned duties.

Years later when he was no longer driving for the school system, we'd bump into one of those kids at the mall or grocery store. And you know what? Not one of them ever forgot him. They recognized him immediately and rushed over to give him a huge bear hug. I think that's what they did best, just about every one of them. They were great at loving people. They offered hugs and grins freely.

Those terrific kids might never become famous scientists or corporate attorneys, but they are becoming all they can be and enjoying every moment of the process. They are reaching for their dreams the same as everybody else. And along the way, they are sharing their own personal type of hope, joy, and enthusiasm. They are genuine and wonderful blessings to everyone around them, and we thank God for them.

Angie's Dream

When she was a little girl, Angie decided to be a nurse. She loved the idea of taking care of people and helping them. Her pets took the place of real patients. She wrapped their paws in bandages, and they cooperated by whining when she taught them.

"Why not be an animal doctor?" her dad asked, encouraging her dream. "You take such good care of your pets."

"No," Angie told him, knowing even then what she wanted for her life. "I want to take care of people. I want to help them get well."

◆ ❖ ◄○►❖ ◆

Thank you, Lord, for letting me follow my dreams, for opening doors for me and for giving me a nudge in the right direction. Thank you for the joy that comes from being the person I was meant to be. Thank you for making me and for setting me free.

◆ ❖ ◄○►❖ ◆

It was a wonderful dream. As soon as she was old enough, Angie volunteered at the hospital. She enjoyed every task assigned her, even the least pleasant ones.

"God has certainly given you the gift of nursing," one nurse told her, with a huge smile. "I'm looking forward to seeing you become a nurse some day."

"Count on it," Angie told her. But life got in the way. Angie's dad lost his job, and then her mom got very sick. There was no money for school. No way Angie could study nursing. So she got a job to help her family get along. The months and years flew by. Soon Angie found herself married, raising her children, and doing her job as a cashier in a discount store.

It wasn't a bad life. She loved her husband and adored her kids. When her parents could not take care of themselves, she took charge, letting that natural love of nursing flow through her. She cared for her own kids when they became ill. She even helped out once a month at a nearby nursing home, just as a volunteer.

Everybody thought she was a natural nurse.

"It's a gift, dear," one of the women in the nursing home told her. "I can tell, you've got it. A God-given gift. What a shame you never became a nurse."

The years slid past, and mostly Angie didn't mind. There were so many good times. She helped put the kids through school, and they did great. She was exceedingly proud of them. Each followed her dreams. Angie urged them to hang onto those dreams and never let go.

Then one day she woke up and realized that, since the kids had moved out, the house felt empty. There were just the two of them now, she and her husband, Ted. She had free time on her hands. She could develop a hobby, raise a garden, take up knitting, or do crafts. Plenty of things she could do with the extra time.

What kept coming into her mind, though, was silly. She kept thinking that at long last she could study to be a nurse.

"I'm too old," she told herself. "The other students will think I'm crazy. My family will laugh at me. It's a stupid idea." But she couldn't get rid of it. All day long it was in the back of her mind. All night long she prayed about it.

Finally, she told her family about her decision. They didn't laugh. They all hugged her and said, "Go for it!" So she did. The studying didn't come easily, but she was determined. When she became discouraged, she didn't give up. This was her dream, and here was her chance to go after it.

After years of effort, she earned her nursing degree, and her whole family came to applaud and cheer for her. On her first day at work in the hospital where she'd volunteered as a girl, she loved every single moment. With a heart full of thankfulness to God, Angie hummed as she worked. This was her dream come true!

WHO AM I?

Who am I, God?
Who am I meant to be?
Where am I going and
how will I know when
I get there?
What am I meant to do
in this world?
What shall I be
when I grow up?
How will I spend my
days and years?
How many will there be?
So many questions.
What are the answers?
Who knows?
Not me. Not yet.

Meant to Be

I think I was meant to be a writer. I loved to read, and it seemed a natural step to begin writing books since I enjoyed them so much. I dove into books as some people dive into oceans. I lost myself in a book. I was totally absorbed in another world and caught up with other people. When I read *Heidi* as a child, I ate bread and Swiss cheese. Books became part of me.

Throughout my life, I've always written. When I was supposed to be doing homework, I was writing short stories. When I was tucked into bed, I wrote by flashlight and yawned through the next day. When I was at work, I was writing during lunch. I think when God shaped and planned me, he put this hunger in me—a hunger to create words on paper became something more.

The sale of my first story set my heart racing and my spirit dancing. After hundreds of writing sales, each one still sets me alight inside. It's work, of course. I have deadlines to meet, word lengths to count, and revisions to make. It's a job like so many others. But I've found over the years that every other job I take leaves me weary and worn out. Writing, no matter how many hours I spend, energizes me.

One thing I like about writing is the way it just flows from me on good days. Other times each and every word fights against me—those are the tough days. But when the words fit together and pour out, that's when it's magic. My heart fills with joy. My life has shape and substance, meaning and purpose.

Putting words on paper doesn't come naturally for everyone. I've heard of people who struggle for hours to string together a few hundred words. For me the words are beautifully behaved, familiar, and a delight. This is why I'm here and why God made me. I am here to write, to transform thoughts and dreams into words on paper and to translate feelings into stories that touch people's lives.

Once in awhile, a reader writes to me, telling me how much my story meant, and my heart rejoices. There's a spark between two people, an

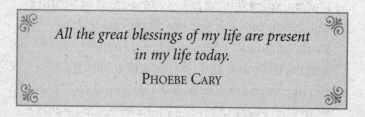

All the great blessings of my life are present in my life today.
PHOEBE CARY

understanding, and a connection. That's what it's all about. That's why there are words on paper. That's why God gives the gift he has given me—the gift of putting words together to make something new and, hopefully, wonderful. That is my dream, my heart's desire—to create with my words something strong and good. It's what God made me to do, and it blesses me and, hopefully, you, too.

* * *

Dear God, I thank you for all that I am and all that I hope someday to be. I thank you for my strengths, for my talents, and for my skills. I thank you for my family and friends. I thank you for all you have given me.

Amen

* * *

Chapter Nine

With God All Things Are Possible

*When we place our trust in God,
our life becomes a miracle
of his making.*

"*T*he life of faith," said Oswald Chambers, a noted Christian writer, "is not the mounting up with wings but a life of walking and not fainting."

God did not create us to fly; he gave that gift to birds. He gave us two feet, two hands, and a soul to discern how to use them. God does not expect us to hover angelically above our work,

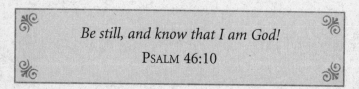

Be still, and know that I am God!

PSALM 46:10

> *When we truly place our faith in God, he fills us with his assurance that we are securely in his hands and that he is in control of each moment of our lives. With peace comes gratitude, for we can't help but thank God for how he is shaping our character and for where he is ultimately taking us.*

trials, and triumphs. Instead, when we trust and believe in our Creator, we can go through our lives expecting miracles because miracles abound in the baking of bread, in the walking in meadows, and in the sitting with a friend.

•◆•◄O►•◆•

In your Word, you say, "Be still, and know that I am God!" But I am making lists of my "to do" lists, and I'm running out of paper. It's hard to find time to be still, and yet I know in stillness you give me strength and in stillness you set my priorities. Please help me find time to be still in you. I want to know you more, Lord.

•◆•◄O►•◆•

Sloshing Through the Parking Lot

The parking lot at the supermarket was full, but I saw a car backing out of a space right next to the parking area for the disabled. I drove what I considered parking lot speed, probably eight miles per hour, toward this unexpected gift on a busy shopping day. Behind me, a motor gunned, tires squealed, and a car full of teenage boys passed me and pulled into "my" parking spot. They were out of the car before I passed their parked car. I was so angry that I was tempted to imitate a scene in the movie *Fried Green Tomatoes* in which a middle-aged woman rams into the sporty car of teenaged girls who had taken "her" parking spot. I recalled what the woman said after an impressive smashing of fenders. "Let's face it, girls. I'm older and better insured."

I finally found a parking spot in what I was now thinking of as "the next state." As I locked the car, the rain began—a real gully washer as we used to say. My

> *Nothing is so strong as gentleness, nothing so gentle as real strength.*
>
> ST. FRANCIS DE SALES

umbrella, hanging in my closet at home, may as well have been in the next state, too. I wondered what the rain would do to my walking cast besides wash away the inscriptions. "You go granny" was already a red and green splotch.

Well, I wouldn't melt. Despite a broken ankle, I was healthy. God was not going to part the waters for me, so I made my way to the store—slowly through puddles because the parking lot was one big puddle, sparing me the need to pioneer a path around them. I was wetter than I had been since my last shower five weeks ago. I had been restricted to sponge baths after I broke my ankle. Nevertheless, it felt good to be wet all over.

By the time I approached the store, the teenagers had finished their shopping. They sped past, splashing more water on me. My first reaction was rage, but then I thought that since I was already soaking wet, how could their thoughtless behavior make me more soaking wet. They hadn't done me any more damage, so why continue to be upset.

The storm was over by the time I left the store, but I knew I had to do something about my cast. My doctor's appointment wasn't until the next week, but I drove right to her office. She took an X-ray, and then she got out a wicked looking drill. "The fracture has healed," she said. "And this cast is coming off. I tell my patients to go home and take a shower but looks like you already had one."

I thought of the teenagers in the parking lot. "Let's face it, boys," I wanted to tell them. "I may be older, and I may be slower, but I'm still insured by God's grace."

<hr/>

PSALM FROM A FAR COUNTRY

The room boy in Nagpur, India,
delivers a wool blanket at 2:00 A.M.
He is barefoot, thin, but clean,
a hustling Indian youth
in hotel uniform.
I am hot.
The window won't open.
The air conditioner is broken.
I was asleep.
Although I am annoyed,
I tip him ten rupees.
But now I am awake,
wondering if an Indian mother prayed
her boy would earn a few rupees for breakfast.
And if God selected me
to put them into his hand.

Slow Train to Mother's

The gift of hospitality is prized in the little Kentucky church where I was raised. The women in the congregation are gracious hostesses especially in times of crisis. They might be surprised that a kind woman in India taught me more about hospitality than they did, perhaps because I badly needed it at the time.

Because I was a resourceful traveler, the thought of taking an overnight train from Bangalore to Chennai was not daunting. The charity I work for has offices in both of these major Indian cities, and I was to present a training session at each. The Bangalore training went well, and a colleague took me to the train station that evening. I purchased a private sleeping compartment.

My colleague escorted me to the door of my compartment and assured me that all I had to do was get off in Chennai, where someone would meet me. He said if I had any problems on the train, just about everyone in India knew a little English.

The air conditioner in the train wasn't working, so I opened the window wide and stretched

> The very word "God" suggests care, kindness,
> goodness; and the idea of God in his infinity is
> infinite care, infinite kindness, infinite goodness.
> We give God the name of good: it is only by
> shortening it that it becomes God.
>
> HENRY WARD BEECHER

out on the plastic pad with my backpack for a
pillow. Soon I was asleep.

In the middle of the night, the train stopped,
and in the moonlight I realized we were stuck in
a noxious swamp. The heat and humidly were
unbearable. So was the stench. I tried to shut the
window, but it stuck. Then mosquitoes attacked.
I covered up with clothes, but they were biting
right through the fabric. I found my bug spray
and sprayed my body, clothes, and even my hair.
Three hours later the train started rolling again.
Soon dust was flying in the window as furiously
as the mosquitoes and stuck to me like a million
tiny magnets thanks to the bug spray.

When I thought we were getting close to
Chennai, I began looking at station signs. They
were in Urdu, not English. I ran down the train
car beating on doors. "English! English!" I cried.
Finally, a door opened, and a woman said she
spoke English. I asked her if she would tell me

when we reached Chennai. "Which station in Chennai?" she asked. She named three.

I prayed desperately and picked one. My prayer was answered. On the station platform stood a young man holding a sign with my name. I staggered toward him, filthy, exhausted, and itching all over. He didn't seem to notice my distress. He just said we would immediately go to the office so I could begin my training session.

I got into the car and burst into tears. He shifted in his seat. He was young, his English was limited, and he didn't know what to do with a wailing woman who was supposed to be a professional trainer. He bit his lip and finally said, "I take you to Mother."

His mother spoke no English, but words were not required. She ran a hot bath for me and poured a lovely scent into the water. She handed me a bar of soap and placed a towel by the tub. While I was drying off, she noticed the huge welts all over my body. Tenderly, she dabbed medicine on me. The itching stopped.

I opened my suitcase and burst into tears again. I had repacked the bug spray without closing the cap. My professional suits were stained and reeking. The mother shrugged and took a pink, silk sari out of her closet and showed me how to turn a rectangle of fabric into a gracious garment. Before I left, she served me tea and a delicious *masala dosa* (rice pancake wrapped around vegetables).

The training session went even better than in Bangalore. I think the staff related to me more easily because I wore a sari, like all of the women in the office did. I thanked God for giving me a new friend, who brought unexpected blessings into my life.

•◦—◦〈O〉◦—◦•

Father, my little boy asked me how to pray.
I told him it was like writing a letter. He got his
pencil and some lined paper. He chewed on the
eraser and then he wrote to you. I know you read
the letter before I did. "Dear God, how are you?"
he wrote. "I am fine." God, thank you that my
child is fine today.

•◦—◦〈O〉◦—◦•

Clemency for a Puppy

My Boston terrier, Bailey, is a surprising answer to a prayer. I've stopped being amazed that prayers are answered, but I certainly shocked myself by asking God to pick out my puppy. Isn't this something I could do alone? Why would

God expect me to seek his help in finding a pet?
My prayer seemed frivolous, but there I was
driving home from work on a snowy January
day, asking God to pick out my puppy. I had
it all planned. I would wait for spring—good
housebreaking weather—and adopt a puppy
from the humane society.

Shortly after my prayer and feeling a little
silly that I had talked to God about a dog, I
noticed a pet store coming up on my right. *Ugh,*
I thought. *Puppy farm.* I had signed petitions
against puppy farms. There were just too many
dogs on death row at humane societies because
no one adopted them. So why was I turning into
the parking lot? *I'll just take a peek,* I thought.
*Get an idea about what kind of dog I'll be looking
for in a few months.*

A half hour later, I was driving home with a
six-week-old Boston terrier zipped inside my
coat with her little, wet nose peeking out. Late
that night, I stood in a sleet storm with a blanket
over my robe while Bailey learned the house
rules. The season was terrible for housebreaking,
but Bailey was irresistibly cute.

A few days later, the vet explained that her
hacking cough was kennel cough requiring
expensive medication and a return visit. The bill

SEE THE SHINING DEWDROPS

See the shining dewdrops
On the flowers strewed,
Proving as they sparkle
"God is ever good."
In the leafy treetops
Where no fears intrude,
Merry birds are singing,
"God is ever good."
Bring my heart, thy tribute—
Songs of gratitude.
All things join to tell us,
"God is ever good,
God is ever good."

was as high as my doctor's bills, and Bailey was not insured. The vet told me that the bulging red membrane on one eye was a "cherry eye." This is a hereditary defect common to Boston terriers, particularly those who have been inbred at puppy farms. It had appeared the day after I had bought her. The surgery would be costly. I was grateful Bailey had an owner who could afford to treat her. Her medical bills would be daunting to a struggling young family, but all I had to do was cut back on my shopping.

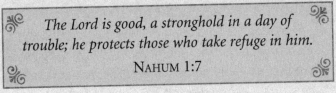

> The Lord is good, a stronghold in a day of trouble; he protects those who take refuge in him.
>
> NAHUM 1:7

I asked the vet what happened to puppies with cherry eye. He said they did not sell. Sadly, they had to be euthanized. On the drive home, Bailey lay curled on her back on the front seat while I scratched her tummy. She wiggled and licked my hand. "Spared by a prayer," I whispered. "Thank you, God."

When the Music Paused

"My life is a symphony," I realized one summer day when the sun seemed to be shining especially for me. After the hard rock and missed beats of raising three teenagers, I was enjoying the even measure of my days. I discovered new joys during the quiet times in my garden and my solitary walks. My spirit would sing uninterrupted by the daily calculus of planning meals that respected my children's politics and health kicks. Sandy was a vegetarian because killing animals is cruel. Jenna refused anything salty

> *Thus says the Lord: Stand at the crossroads, and look, and ask for the ancient paths, where the good way lies; and walk in it, and find rest for your souls.*
>
> JEREMIAH 6:16

because she was convinced it would give her high blood pressure. And Dan, who had written a term paper on pesticides, insisted that if we put anything in our refrigerator that was not certified "organic," our genes would mutate.

But one day, the music stopped. My walks became stomps around the neighborhood. My garden still bloomed, but I bemoaned the weeds more than I rejoiced in the begonias. My God, who had steered me through motherhood with a steady hand, had abandoned my Sandy. That gentle young woman, so kind that she refused to eat meat slaughtered for the table, had been cruelly dumped by the man she had loved for three years. I had prayed for her happiness every day of my life. In the first few months of her sorrow, I continued to pray, trusting that God would send her another man, and this time one who truly loved her. I walked and prayed, gardened and prayed, with great faith, hope, and trust.

Then I got mad.

I was so mad at God that I refused to hear the symphony of his creation that I finally had time to enjoy. I was so frustrated and furious that I finally told Sandy that I was mad at God and could no longer pray. I told

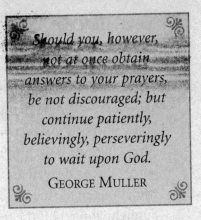

Should you, however, not at once obtain answers to your prayers, be not discouraged; but continue patiently, believingly, perseveringly to wait upon God.

GEORGE MULLER

her that I had prayed for her and prayed for her, but nothing was changing. "God is deaf," I told her.

I waited for lightening to strike, but instead, Sandy just looked at me over the vegetarian stew she had prepared and said, "Mom, maybe you're praying for the wrong person. God and I are doing just fine."

Driving home I thought about Sandy and her vegetarian kitchen, Jenna and her salt-free table, Dan and his strictly organic meals. I thought about the pork chops in my freezer, the pretzels in my pantry, and the pesticides that kept my homegrown tomatoes pristine. My children are responsible for their own meals, their own music, and their own prayers. God showed me that he was taking good care of them, and I was thankful.

Over My Shoulder

The traffic out of Miami was heavy that day, and cars were exceeding the speed limit in all four lanes. I needed to ease over a lane before exiting. After checking both mirrors, I began to turn the wheel. Just as my van approached the lane line, something made me look over my shoulder. Sunlight glinted off the fender of a car driving beside me that the mirrors had not reflected. I straightened the wheel, and when I could, I moved over and exited, still shaking all over.

I drove into a little park beside a lagoon to compose myself. Although I had more errands than time that afternoon, the verdant peacefulness was too inviting to ignore. I dangled my feet in the cool water and thought about what caused me to look over my shoulder. Then I thought about my husband's deep faith in God

An egret strutting around his mate reminded me of a past event. I had been reading a menu outside the Atlantic Café thinking that a lonely

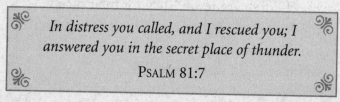

In distress you called, and I rescued you; I answered you in the secret place of thunder.

PSALM 81:7

vacation was better than no vacation but not much better. "Would you like something to eat?" asked a deep, interesting voice. Ordinarily I ignore such offers from strangers, and I walk away. But something made me turn my head. The man looked so kind and trustworthy that I nodded my head. What began with swordfish continues today over shredded wheat and midnight raids on the pantry.

The egrets flew away, and I remembered my errands. My shoes were still hot, but I felt so cool and refreshed that I no longer dreaded the crowded mall. As I buckled my seat belt, I wondered where I would be now if I had not looked over my shoulder outside the Atlantic Café and, more frighteningly, just moments ago on the highway.

The next day as my husband left for church, he looked over his shoulder as usual to ask, "Are you sure you won't come with me?" But this time he smiled before he spoke, for I was standing by the door with the car keys in my hand.

Dear God, show me the way that I should go today. I have many choices, yet I know there is just one way that will bring me closer to you. Thank you, Lord, for that way. Amen

Chapter Ten

The Gift of Humor

The priceless gift of laughter has the power to heal the body, mind, and spirit.

*T*here is something simply magical about looking at life from a different perspective. Often, we find that things are not as bad as they first seemed. Sometimes, we even find something to laugh about when we see things from this new angle.

A sense of humor is the ability to see the lighter side of life, even when events on the outside don't seem joyful and simple. Learning to laugh at ourselves and the world around us becomes a powerful tool for personal healing

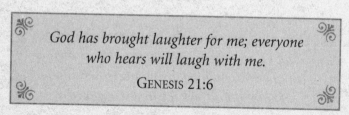

God has brought laughter for me; everyone who hears will laugh with me.

GENESIS 21:6

and the ability to help others feel better about themselves. Without a good sense of humor, life would be dry and dull and filled with drudgery.

Anything can evoke a bit of humor if looked at with fresh eyes and a sense of awe and wonder. From a child's silly antics to a colleague's whispered joke, from a funny story on the evening news to a goofy picture e-mailed from a caring friend, there is plenty to laugh about in this crazy, chaotic world. When we seek out the things that make us laugh, we are always ready to take on the darker, tougher times, for when we do, God equips us with a foundation of joy and wisdom.

Laughter is the best medicine, somebody wise and witty once said, and laughter in large doses can help cure even the worst of illnesses. God must have wanted us to laugh and to make each other laugh, or why else would he have given us funny bones?

＊◈━◇━◈＊

God, thank you for the blessing of humor and for my ability to laugh at my faults, failures, and foibles. Thank you for reminding me not to take myself, and my life, too seriously.

＊◈━◇━◈＊

Something to Laugh At

My mom somehow seemed to know things that others couldn't possibly discern. When she was diagnosed with terminal cancer, she had already told several relatives what she suspected. She had even badgered her doctor with her unwarranted suspicions. Despite the terrible news and the fear it inspired in those of us who loved her, her reaction was to smile at her doctor and say, "Told you so!"

My mom had a surprising sense of humor; surprising because, despite her petite size and her sweet face, she could fire off an outrageous joke or a hilarious limerick. She was never afraid to use her sense of humor to put someone else in their place, especially me and my two brothers. Mom just loved to zing out the zingers, but always with love and a spirit of fun.

Watching her go through chemo and surgery, and hearing the heart-breaking news that it had

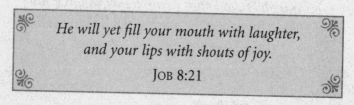

He will yet fill your mouth with laughter,
and your lips with shouts of joy.

JOB 8:21

Just a simple change in our perspective can help us find the humor in any difficult or chaotic event. By looking at life with a grateful spirit and an open mind, we are sure to see the lighter side to every dark situation and the potential for laughter even as our heart breaks with sadness.

not stopped the cancer ravaging her body, my mom called me and my siblings to her side and told us she was certain she was going to die. We were devastated, to say the least, although we had already received her diagnosis from her surgeon and doctors. But hearing it come directly from her made it much more real.

She watched us cry and reach out to hold her, and once she had enough, she told us the jokes she had pried out of the nurses and doctors. We started to laugh through our tears, unable to help ourselves, thinking that she was just covering her pain with these attempts at humor. But watching her over the next few days proved otherwise. She seemed very much at peace with God and willing to share a good laugh or two. I had to sit down with her one night and ask her if she was just in denial of her fate. She looked at me with utter surprise and said something I will never forget.

"Honey, if I leave this world teaching you just one thing I learned from God, let it be this: Life is meaningless without something to laugh at."

She passed away the next day with a room filled with family, friends, and the nurses and doctors who had come to adore her and her witty lust for life. No one present in that room, indeed present in her life, would ever forget the power that humor had to help make her transition a much more peaceful one, for her as well as for us. And all of us who continued to carry on without her did so with a much greater sense of joy and a real gratitude for the blessings of laughter that God gives us each and every day.

* —◄○►— *

STOP, LOOK, LAUGH!

No matter how much I am hurting
Or how terrible life seems to be,
I can always find something to laugh at
If I stop thinking so seriously.
When everything seems so distressful
Or that nothing I do seems worthwhile,
It is only a matter of time before God
Gives me something to make my heart smile.

* —◄○►— *

The Protest

Jen's day just couldn't get any worse. Everything that could have gone wrong did go wrong, which reminded her of Murphy's Law as she tried to clean up a work disaster that had cost the company a great deal of time and money.

She sat at her computer, crying and glad that her boss and colleagues had gone home. It would be a long night for her, working at her desk and trying to find a way to undo a mistake that she herself had signed off on. It was her fault; she had not read the paperwork as closely as she should have, although her boss was responsible for approving her "approvals." Still, Jen took the brunt of the blame, and she accepted responsibility for it like a trouper.

Convinced she would lose her job, Jen resigned herself to just getting through the night with her sanity in tact. She ordered food to be delivered to the reception desk out front and dug in for the long haul.

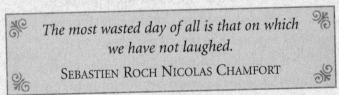

The most wasted day of all is that on which we have not laughed.

SEBASTIEN ROCH NICOLAS CHAMFORT

ANGELS OF GOOD CHEER

Blessed are those who see humor
In even the toughest of things
And who always find something to laugh about
No matter what suffering brings.
For these are the angels of laughter
Who come bearing gifts of good cheer
And who know how to brighten each moment
With joyfulness, comfort, and care.
For blessed are those who find something
That makes the heart happily dream
And who always find something to thank God for
No matter how bleak life may seem.

The next day, after three hours of sleep and a quick shower, Jen was sitting with her boss, listening with a sense of detachment as he told her that she was being demoted. As she left his office, she was conflicted, feeling anger at being demoted but gratitude for not being fired. She checked her e-mail and found one from her friend and colleague, April. When she read it, she wondered what on earth April was up to.

"Protest at noon on County Courthouse steps. Rescind Murphy's Law. Meet you there!"

Jen chuckled, knowing April's sense of silly humor, and then turned her attention to other things. But at about 15 minutes to noon, April showed up at Jen's office and demanded that Jen take an early lunch to go to this "protest." Jen figured, why not? and went along. Soon she was shocked to find that April was indeed driving to the County Courthouse! After they parked and got out, April opened her trunk, removing two big picket signs.

Jen gasped when she saw the signs, which read: RESCIND MURPHY'S LAW! EVERYTHING THAT CAN GO RIGHT WILL GO RIGHT!

April grabbed her hand and the two of them spent the next hour protesting Murphy's Law as a huge crowd gathered. Soon, local TV cameras showed up, and the two women laughed and chanted, "Down with Murphy's Law!" and explained their "cause" to the smiling news media and onlookers. When they returned to their offices, their fellow colleagues were cheering them on as they walked in. Even Jen's boss was laughing, and later he told Jen that he was glad she was still on the team and that he would give her every opportunity for future advancement.

Jen later thanked April for realizing just how much of a perspective-change she had needed. Her friend's unyielding sense of humor and her

Christian spirit had made all the difference in Jen's attitude. She was now ready to work hard, aim high, and believe that everything that could go right indeed would with God leading the way.

God, today has been really tough with so many difficult challenges. I often feel discouraged until I remember the many blessings you have given me, including my wonderful sense of humor. All I need to do is find something, however small, to laugh at, and I feel renewed again.

Funny Face

Brian sat in the subway train, his newspaper propped up to shield him from having to face any other human beings. After all, he was just told that his performance level at his job was not enough to warrant his being employed. In other words, he was fired.

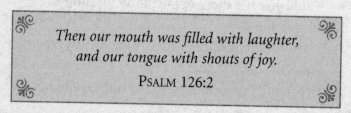

Then our mouth was filled with laughter, and our tongue with shouts of joy.

PSALM 126:2

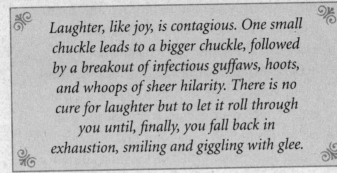

Laughter, like joy, is contagious. One small chuckle leads to a bigger chuckle, followed by a breakout of infectious guffaws, hoots, and whoops of sheer hilarity. There is no cure for laughter but to let it roll through you until, finally, you fall back in exhaustion, smiling and giggling with glee.

He had hated selling insurance, not because it was a terrible job, but because he had never been good at talking and persuading others to buy something they didn't necessarily want. During the past year, he felt unhappy with his job, and it reflected in job performance.

Now, he was back to square one, with only a one month severance and a few months' worth of salary in savings to help make the new job search a little less desperate. Still, he felt lost, empty, and totally unsure of where God could be leading him, and it was a feeling he hated.

He could hear the soft giggles of a child across from where he sat, and he managed a glimpse from out behind his fortress of daily news. Sitting directly across from him was a little toddler, a boy of about maybe three or four, staring at Brian and making faces. Beside the child was a young woman reading a magazine, evidently the child's mother, and Brian felt a slight sense of irritation that she was unaware of her little boy's behavior.

Back behind the safety of the local business pages, Brian rolled his eyes while the little boy's giggles once again disrupted his escape from reality. He peeked out at the child, who was now mugging at Brian with a series of facial contortions fit for a circus performer. This time, Brian stuck his tongue out in retaliation, thereby launching a full-scale funny face attack. For the next half hour, Brian waged goofy face war with the little toddler, and soon everyone in the subway car was joining in. Even the woman beside the child laughed.

As Brian left the subway train at his stop, he was almost sorry to go. He gave the child one more google-eyed, cheek twist and then walked the rest of the way home smiling from ear to ear in a better mood than he had been in months. After he got home, he turned on the TV and began to prepare himself a nice dinner, still feeling happy from his subway hijinks.

Brian was delighted when he discovered that *The Mask* with Jim Carrey was scheduled for the evening. He had to laugh again at the prevalence of funny faces throughout his day. Surely, he thought, God was trying to tell him something, and with a big ham sandwich in his hand, Brian sat down to spend the next two hours laughing at what he thought was a very entertaining movie. Even though he was jobless, Brian felt hopeful, even somewhat excited, about the possibilities that lay just ahead.

But for now, there was ham and cheese and a whole lot of laughter God had blessed him with.

* ❖ ❖ ⟨O⟩ ❖ ❖ *

Dear Lord, give me the strength and the insight to see the lighter side of this messy situation. Let me find a reason to laugh amidst the pain and a reason to smile even though I feel like crying. Help me find my funny bone again.

* ❖ ❖ ⟨O⟩ ❖ ❖ *

Laughter in the Dark

Alice had done just what the federal emergency workers had told her to do to secure her mobile home from the powerful winds they were expecting. A strong storm system was moving in with the potential for spawning tornadoes, and Alice had followed all the directions for reinforcing windows and battening down the

> *A good laugh is sunshine in the house.*
> WILLIAM MAKEPEACE THACKERY

hatches. She had wanted to evacuate, but the thought of leaving the only thing she owned, her mobile home, made her sick to her stomach.

Although most of her neighbors had left for Red Cross shelters, Alice chose to stay behind and go down with the ship if she had to. Her next-door neighbor, Sheila, a feisty elderly

---

A MEDITATION FOR LAUGHTER
No matter how hard this day may be,
I can laugh.
No matter how much my body may hurt,
I can laugh.
No matter how tough my financial situation is,
I can laugh.
No matter how tired and weary I feel,
I can laugh.
No matter how difficult my relationship has been,
I can laugh.
Laughter is the healing balm that soothes
the aches and pains of my body,
my mind, and my spirit.

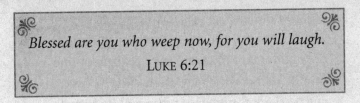

Blessed are you who weep now, for you will laugh.

LUKE 6:21

woman, had also decided to stick around, and she and Alice got together in Alice's reinforced shelter room, which her husband had built before he had passed away. They played cards by candlelight when the power went out and munched on chips and root beer as the winds and rain howled outside like screaming banshees on the loose.

When a tornado descended upon their mobile home park, Alice and Sheila prayed and held each other as that horrible train wreck sound echoed off the walls, moving closer until the entire mobile home shook on its foundation. As the mobile home rocked violently, Alice and Sheila struggled to keep their footing, but then the mobile home turned on its side, and their arms and legs wildly thrashed the air.

The main brunt of the tornado moved past them, but Alice and Sheila could hear the monster ripping into other homes nearby, tearing up roofs and walls like a cat clawing up weeds in the grass. After what seemed like an eternity, there was an eerie silence outside. Rescue teams arrived and were surprised to hear the sound of laughter coming from the darkness of one mobile home, which lay on its side. As two rescue workers climbed atop the mobile home and pried open the door, which was now facing skyward, they smiled at the sight revealed by their powerful flashlights: two elderly ladies sitting in a pile of potato chips, laughing and thanking God that they were still alive.

He'll Be Fine!

Wanda sat in the hospital waiting room, weeping softly and asking God to cure her husband of 40 years. Jim had suffered a serious heart attack and was going to have surgery to clean out some seriously blocked arteries. The surgery was tricky because of the proximity of the suspected arteries to the heart, and Wanda had been told to consider the chance that Jim might not make it.

It was not an option Wanda wanted to consider, but she knew she would have to stop denying the possibility that she would spend her retirement alone. It seemed to her that she and

> *Let all who seek you rejoice and be glad in you. Let those who love your salvation say evermore, "God is great!"*
>
> PSALM 70:4

Jim had loved each other forever, sharing life in all its ups and downs, laughing and playing and working together for a future they might not ever achieve. She could feel her heart breaking.

When her daughter Sandra showed up, Wanda allowed her to stay at the hospital long enough for her to go home, change her clothes, and pack a few things. She was determined to sleep at the hospital and not leave Jim's side, no matter what the outcome of the surgery. She wanted to be there if he made it, and she wanted even more so to be there if he didn't.

Back at the hospital, Wanda fearfully listened as Sandra told her that Jim's surgeon was immediately starting the operation. Sandra took her mom to the waiting area for the long night ahead. The two of them napped on the couch, taking turns to retrieve snacks and coffee. Soon, the light of a new day made itself obvious, and Sandra offered to run out and get some fresh things for the two of them. As Wanda waited,

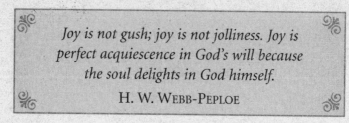

Joy is not gush; joy is not jolliness. Joy is perfect acquiescence in God's will because the soul delights in God himself.

H. W. WEBB-PEPLOE

two of Jim's doctors came out to talk with her. By the looks on their faces, Wanda felt reassured.

The doctors reported that Jim had come through the surgery with flying colors and would make a full recovery. They warned her, however, that the healing process would be something she and Jim would have to take very seriously. Wanda vowed to do whatever they suggested to help her husband become better. As they rose to leave, one of them smiled and said, "Don't worry; he'll be fine!" His words helped her feel that Jim was going to recover. Still, she wouldn't really believe it until she could see him with her own eyes.

When Wanda entered the hospital room, she was totally unprepared for what she was about to see. Jim's surgery had been serious, even dangerous, and she knew he would be, at the very least, completely exhausted, if even awake. She approached his bedside with great apprehension, ready to face his condition with a strong heart and a hopeful spirit.

Instead, she broke out into a howl of outrageous laughter. Jim, her one true love and her best friend and partner in life, lay in bed wearing a pair of sunglasses. Weakly and with great effort, he lifted his hand to his mouth and pretended to wiggle a cigar at Wanda, who was beside herself with tears of joy streaming down her cheeks.

That's when she thanked God for the blessing of a good, healthy laugh and for giving her a second chance at a life filled with laughter with her beloved husband, Jim.

—◇—

Holy Spirit, fill me with light and laughter so that I may be a beacon of hope, cheer, and optimism to all those I encounter today. Remind me of life's lighter side that I may serve as a reminder to others lost in the darkness. Thank you for the joy you have firmly planted in my heart, knowing that your love for me is an eternal gift.
Amen

—◇—

Marie D. Jones is an ordained minister and a contributing author to numerous books, including *Sisters, Mother, Grandmother, Friends, Graduation, Wedding, A Mother's Daily Prayer Book, When You Lose Someone You Love: A Year of Comfort,* and *God's Answers to Tough Questions.*

Karen Leet is a freelance writer who has a Masters in modern literature. Her inspirational stories and articles are published by a variety of national publications, including *Christian Reader, Evangel, Sunday Digest,* and *Today's Christian Woman.*

Carol Stigger is an award-winning communications consultant, writing teacher, and freelance writer. Her inspirational work appears in several national magazines and newspapers, including *Christian Science Monitor, Guideposts, Chicago Tribune, Vital Christianity,* and *Providence Journal.* She is also author of *Opportunity Knocks.*